P9-EME-379

The Spanish-American War: "Remember the Maine!"
Robert Somerlott
AR B.L.: 8.1
Points: 4.0   MG

THE SPANISH-AMERICAN WAR

Titles in the American War Series

The American Revolution
"Give Me Liberty, or
Give Me Death!"
Paperback 0-7660-1727-3
Library Ed. 0-89490-521-X

The Civil War
"A House Divided"
Paperback 0-7660-1728-1
Library Ed. 0-89490-522-8

The Korean War
"The Forgotten War"
Paperback 0-7660-1729-X
Library Ed. 0-89490-526-0

The Mexican War
"Mr. Polk's War"
Library Ed. 0-7660-1853-9

The Persian Gulf War
"The Mother of All Battles"
Paperback 0-7660-1730-3
Library Ed. 0-89490-528-7

The Spanish-American War
"Remember the Maine!"
Library Ed. 0-7660-1855-5

The War of 1812
"We Have Met the Enemy and
They Are Ours"
Library Ed. 0-7660-1854-7

World War I
"The War to End Wars"
Paperback 0-7660-1732-X
Library Ed. 0-89490-523-6

World War II
in Europe
"America Goes to War"
Paperback 0-7660-1733-8
Library Ed. 0-89490-525-2

World War II
in the Pacific
"Remember Pearl Harbor"
Paperback 0-7660-1734-6
Library Ed. 0-89490-524-4

The Vietnam War
"What Are We Fighting For?"
Paperback 0-7660-1731-1
Library Ed. 0-89490-527-9

T 31920

L

THE SPANISH-AMERICAN WAR

"Remember the Maine!"

Robert Somerlott

Enslow Publishers, Inc.

40 Industrial Road	PO Box 38
Box 398	Aldershot
Berkeley Heights, NJ 07922	Hants GU12 6BP
USA	UK

http://www.enslow.com

"Remember the Maine!"
—Slogan in the Spanish-American War, 1898

Copyright © 2002 by Robert Somerlott

All rights reserved.

No part of this book may be reproduced by any means
without the written permission of the publisher.

Library of Congress Cataloging-in-Publication Data

Somerlott, Robert.
  The Spanish-American War : "Remember the Maine!" / Robert Somerlott.
    p. cm. — (American war series)
  Includes bibliographical references (p.) and index.
  ISBN-10: 0-7660-1855-5
  1. Spanish-American War, 1898—Juvenile literature. [1. Spanish-American
War, 1898.] I. Title. II. Series.
  E715 .S76 2002
  973.8'9—dc21

                                    2001004118

ISBN-13: 978-0-7660-1855-6

Printed in the United States of America

10 9 8 7 6 5 4 3

To Our Readers:
We have done our best to make sure all Internet Addresses in this book were
active and appropriate when we went to press. However, the author and the
publisher have no control over and assume no liability for the material
available on those Internet sites or on other Web sites they may link to. Any
comments or suggestions can be sent by e-mail to comments@enslow.com or
to the address on the back cover.

Illustration Credits: AP/Wide World Photos, p. 109; Dictionary of
American Portraits, published by Dover Publications, Inc., in 1967, pp. 14,
16, 30, 60, 82, 99, 113; Enslow Publishers, Inc., pp. 22, 26, 41, 46, 48, 68,
92, 96; The John F. Kennedy Library, p. 110; Library of Congress, pp. 24,
72, 90; Organization of American States, p. 28; National Archives, pp. 10,
19, 39, 56, 76, 78, 86, 100, 102.

Cover Illustration: National Archives, chromolithograph of Theodore
Roosevelt and the Rough Riders.

Contents

Foreword

The following excerpt is from a speech given by Senator Redfield Proctor of Vermont in the U.S. Senate on March 17, 1898. It was delivered about a month after the sinking of the U.S.S. *Maine* in Havana harbor, and before war was declared. Proctor's eyewitness account expressed the horrid conditions in Cuba under Spanish rule. He hoped to illustrate the effects of the reconcentration policy, a program of driving Cuban civilians into fortified towns in order to contain "rebels". The movement of the Cuban population, cattle, and food was strongly controlled during this time leading to starvation and disease.

It is not within the narrow limits of my vocabulary to portray it. I went to Cuba with a strong conviction that the picture had been overdrawn; that a few cases of starvation and suffering had inspired and stimulated the press correspondents, and that they had given free play to a strong, natural and highly cultivated imagination.

I could not believe that out of a population of one million six hundred thousand, 200,000 had died within these Spanish forts, practically prison walls, within a few months past, from actual starvation and disease caused by insufficient and improper food.

My inquiries were entirely outside of sensational sources. They were made by our medical officers, of our consuls, of city alcaldes [mayors], of relief commitees, of leading merchants and bankers, physicians and lawyers. Several of my informants were Spanish born, but every time came the answer that the case had not been overstated.

What I saw I cannot tell so that others can see it. It must be seen with one's own eyes to be realized.

There are many things worse than war. It may be that the United States is to become the Knight Errant of the world. War with Spain may put her in a position to demand civil and religious liberty for the oppressed of every nation and of every clime.

—Methodist bishop Charles C. McCabe at the onset of the Spanish-American War

1 Explosion in Havana

The U.S. battleship *Maine* rested at anchor in the harbor of Havana, Cuba, on the night of February 15, 1898. The *Maine* was a sleek vessel, its gray steel gleaming faintly in cloudy moonlight. Aboard were 354 American sailors. A few were on guard duty, patrolling the decks, alert but silent. Boxes of ammunition had been placed near the one- and six-pound guns, ready for quick reloading in case of attack.

Captain Charles S. Sigsbee, who had sailed the *Maine* into the Havana harbor two weeks before, felt he was on a risky mission. He had "sensed danger" and taken precautions. His ship was ready for quick action.[1] Yet tonight there was not the least sign of trouble. Nothing disturbed the quiet harbor.

7

At nine o'clock the ship's bell rang the hour. The *Maine*'s bugler played taps—the final bugle command of the day and the signal for "lights out." As it turned out, this bugle call was the last ever to be sounded on the deck of the American ship.

The air was a bit hazy that evening. Captain Sigsbee noticed that the thin mist was interrupted by bright tropical star constellations.[2] He would see clearly if any suspicious boats approached the *Maine*.

Captain Sigsbee could make out the forbidding stone tower of Moro Castle, dark against the sky, across the bay. The castle, built long ago to defend Havana against pirates or other invaders, loomed as a symbol of the once-mighty power of Spain. Once, Spain had boasted the greatest empire in the world, controlling most of Central and South America. Some former Spanish colonies—Mexico, Argentina, Peru, and a dozen other Latin American countries—had become independent nations. Cuba still remained under Spanish control, but the island was struggling—without success so far—to gain its freedom.

In 1895, after decades of futile revolt, a simmering Cuba erupted into a full-scale war for independence. Spanish reaction was swift and brutal. Lines of blockhouses—small easily defended buildings—and barbed wire fences were built across the narrow parts of the island. Most of the farming population, consisting of thousands of civilians, was held in detention camps as Cuba bristled with bayonets and violence. On the island, killings and starvation were rampant.

A weakened Spain had lost many of its vast possessions, but some islands—including the Philippines and Puerto Rico—were still held by the Spanish Crown. A large area in North Africa also remained under Spain's control.

Cuba, Spain's oldest large colony in the New World, was still its proudest possession. Centuries ago, Spanish adventurers had launched their great conquests from Cuba, seizing Mexico, Central America, and most of the huge South American continent.

The damp stone dungeons of Moro Castle had once held rebels and traitors against Spain, who were brought to Havana for punishment. There was a torture chamber, which housed a heavy chair used to hold prisoners being executed by strangulation. The castle fortress remained a terrifying place to anyone who resisted Spanish rule.

If Moro Castle was a symbol of ancient Spanish power, then the *Maine* reflected the military force of the modern United States. In its hold were torpedoes, and the ship was loaded with artillery, including guns powerful enough to blast down the whole Havana waterfront. One officer, boasting of the ship's weapons, once said, "We have Havana at our mercy."[3]

The *Maine* had been sent to Cuba to display American military power. Its official mission was to protect the lives and property of American citizens in Cuba. If the violent revolution in the island's countryside should spill over into Havana, Captain Sigsbee and his men stood ready to intervene and evacuate any Americans in danger. So far, the Cuban capital seemed quiet and safe,

Captain Charles S. Sigsbee sailed the U.S. battleship *Maine* into the Havana harbor in January 1898.

and Spanish officials privately ridiculed the American fears of riots in Havana, resenting the presence of a foreign battleship in their harbor.

Cuba lies only ninety miles from Florida, making it one of America's closest neighbors. For months, a segment of the people in the United States had been angrily protesting Spain's treatment of the Cuban people during their struggle for independence. Horror stories appeared in American newspapers: accounts of torture, murder, and starvation. Some of these reports had been exaggerated, but others were all too true.

An investigator sent to Cuba by the U.S. government claimed that a full third of the rural population of Cuba had already died as the result of war, imprisonment, and starvation.[4]

William McKinley, president of the United States, hoped that American outrage would not lead to actual war—at least not yet. He claimed America should not be "plunged into war until we are ready for it."[5] McKinley also said that if he could avoid war, he would be the happiest man in the world. He had already seen too much bloodshed in the American Civil War.

The president's words rejecting war, however, also seemed to suggest that war was very possible. Sending the battleship *Maine* to Havana was a strong warning to the Spaniards that the United States cared deeply about the inhumane events taking place so close to its border.

Captain Sigsbee felt no alarm as he stood at the railing of the *Maine* for what would be the last time and listened to some crewman playing a mandolin in the darkness of the ship.[6] He also heard distant music that night. Along the Havana waterfront stood outdoor cafes where people gathered in the evening for supper, to drink, or to chat. If they were lucky, they also enjoyed a cooling night breeze from the sea. Captain Sigsbee could see twinkling lights near these cafe tables as music floated softly across a mile of dark water.[7]

Two Reporters

On Havana's waterfront, two American journalists, who were becoming famous in Cuba, were seated at a cafe table. George Bronson Rea wrote about Cuba for the *New York Herald.* His companion, Sylvester Scovel, was a reporter for another New York newspaper, the *World.* Both men had traveled extensively throughout Cuba. Likewise, both had watched recent events closely and talked to countless native people. But they had reached very different conclusions regarding Cuba's current conditions.

Rea believed that American newspapers were printing lies to boost their circulation, and trying to "embroil the U.S. in a war with Spain."[8] He was especially angry about accounts that the Spanish authorities had been "feeding Cuban prisoners to the sharks" near Moro Castle. "It never happened," he said, pronouncing such reports "rot."[9] In Rea's view, "too much sympathy has been wasted on the Cuban rebellion."[10] The reporter blamed both sides for crimes that had been committed and described General Máximo Gómez, the leader of the rebels, as "a withered old man who gave one the idea of a resurrected Egyptian mummy."[11] Scovel believed almost the opposite. He declared: "Extermination of the Cuban people under the cloak of civilized warfare is Spain's settled purpose."[12]

While in Cuba, the two men had shared many dangerous and life-threatening experiences in the mountains and jungles. They had become friends, and tonight, as they sat looking at the quiet harbor, they could clearly see the *Maine* at anchor in the distance. No boats were approaching the vessel, and it did not worry the reporters that armed American sailors were on guard pacing the decks.

A few minutes later, a terrible explosion shattered the night. The windows of the cafe were blown out, spraying the reporters with broken glass. Running into the waterfront street, they saw flames rising from where they had earlier seen the *Maine*. Scovel later wrote that "the harbor was lit up with intense light and above it could be seen innumerable colored lights resembling rockets."[13]

Clara Barton in Havana

One of America's most admired women was in Havana that night, working where she had a clear view of the harbor. This woman was Clara Barton, the founder of the American Red Cross and the great reformer of military hospitals. She had gained fame during the Civil War, becoming known as the Angel of the Battlefield.

Barton had studied the U.S. government report describing the starvation, poverty, and lack of medical care in Cuba. This pushed her into action, sending

Barton directly to the White House to see the president. McKinley named her as head of a volunteer committee to aid the Cubans.

Six months later, Barton and a Spanish translator arrived in Havana with food and medical supplies. Barton found the Spanish officials polite but unhelpful as she inspected hospital conditions and sought bakers to help turn flour into bread.

At this time, thousands of Cubans with suspected rebel sympathies were imprisoned by the Spanish

Clara Barton was named head of a volunteer committee to aid Cubans by President William McKinley.

government in concentration camps. These prisoners faced starvation, and Clara Barton begged the Havana authorities to allow the captives to plant crops inside the fences that confined them. The Spaniards listened to her with grave sympathy, nodded, and did nothing.[14]

What Barton found in Cuba horrified her. She saw starvation and suffering everywhere. She had never seen such cruelty as she discovered in Cuba, and it seemed to her that the Spanish government was to blame.

Now another of Barton's long days of work was ending. She looked out at the harbor and saw the *Maine* standing at anchor in the calm water. Barton was finishing up when a terrible explosion shook the windows of the room. Barton later wrote, "The deafening roar was a burst of thunder as perhaps one never heard before. And off to the right, out over the bay, the air was filled with a blaze of light."[15]

The World Explodes

Aboard the *Maine*, Captain Sigsbee had heard the three chimes that signaled nine-thirty. He spent the next ten minutes finishing a letter to his wife. Just as he had folded the page and was putting it into an envelope, a blast rocked the ship.

There were two explosions, one rapidly after the other. Within a second or two, a rain of objects fell from overhead: fragments of steel railings, lumps of cement, blocks of wood. Some of the crew were knocked down and injured by the flying debris. Others never awoke in their bunk beds and hammocks, killed by the blast as they slept. Some ran toward the deck to take battle stations or to begin launching boats, as the ship was rapidly sinking.

Captain Sigsbee, the letter to his wife still in his hand, heard "a bursting, rending, crashing roar of immense volume."[16] He felt the ship lurch and tip. All lights went out and smoke poured into his cabin. As Sigsbee struggled in the darkness, the ship tilted sharply and the captain had to crawl through a porthole to reach the main deck. A sailor described him standing there calmly, "as cool as if at a ball."[17]

Captain Sigsbee, not knowing what might happen next, shouted to the crew to prepare to ward off any hostile boarders attempting to get onto the *Maine*. He then

Captain Sigsbee attempted to remain calm during the *Maine* explosion despite confusion as to what had caused the incident.

realized that there was almost no one left to obey the order and actually not much left to protect. The *Maine* was a hopeless wreck.

Sigsbee believed his ship had been mysteriously attacked. Perhaps a torpedo had struck it; perhaps some fort on shore had fired a cannon. He could not, at the time, explain it.

Parts of the ship had burst into flame. By the light of the fires, Sigsbee could see that the *Maine* had already become a twisted mass of metal. As he splashed through the water rapidly rising on the deck, Sigsbee believed he heard cheers on the distant shore.[18] He then ordered the few remaining lifeboats quickly lowered to rescue the "white forms" of sailors, whether living or dead, from the dark waters of Havana harbor.

By this time, reporters Scovel and Rea had found a boat and were rowing toward the sinking ship. When they approached the area of the explosion, Rea described the scene: "The bow had disappeared. The foremast and smokestacks had fallen, and to add to the horror, the mass of wreckage amidships was on fire."[19]

Clara Barton wasted no time looking at the harbor. She hurried to the large Havana hospital, San Ambrosio, where "thirty to forty" of the wounded *Maine* sailors had been taken. "They had been crushed by timbers, cut by iron, scorched by fire."[20] Since the Spanish doctors seemed to have the terrible scene under control, Barton began to take down the names and addresses of the wounded. Most of the victims were either already dead or were on the verge of dying.

A Secret Agent Sends News

In the wake of the disaster, Spanish authorities halted telegraph messages from Havana. Reporter Scovel, who had stolen a blank cable, managed to get about a hundred words to the Associated Press, a company that gathers news for many American newspapers. The first solid news came from a Cuban agent working secretly for American naval intelligence in Havana. Soon after ten o'clock in Key West, Florida, the telegraph receiver began clicking, alerting Americans that the *Maine* had been sunk.

No one could quite believe this first report, but then a clear message came in from Captain Sigsbee: "*Maine* blown up in Havana harbor at nine forty tonight and destroyed. Many wounded and doubtless more killed or drowned."[21]

"This Means War"

About two hours later in New York City, William Randolph Hearst, owner and publisher of the *New York Journal,* received a message about the explosion in Havana. For months, Hearst had been printing horror stories, both true and false, about events in Cuba. Often, he had been accused of promoting an armed struggle between Spain and the United States. Now, he asked the night editor what would be on the front page of their newspaper besides articles about the *Maine* explosion.

"Only the other big news," replied the editor.

"There is not any other big news," said Hearst. "Please spread the story all over the page. This means war!"[22]

The *Maine* (pictured), once a symbol of American military force, was completely destroyed after the explosion.

I have been through one war; I have seen the dead piled up, and I do not want to see another.
   —President William McKinley to Captain Leonard Wood

2 "Remember the *Maine*"

The war that publisher William Randolph Hearst was looking forward to did not immediately follow the *Maine* disaster. The sinking of the ship was such a dramatic event that many Americans believed that the war broke out at once. Actually, a long political struggle between those wanting war and those hoping for peace continued for weeks, the outcome uncertain. The *Maine* incident, however, had a powerful and lasting effect on American public opinion.

War fever swept across the United States. News of the death count—266 American sailors were killed in the blast—fueled the outrage. Within a few days, the explosion seemed to echo in every part of the angry country. Newspapers owned by Hearst were, as usual, among the

20

most rabid. Some developed a war slogan that quickly spread across the country:

"Remember the *Maine*, to Hell with Spain."[1]

President McKinley, trying to keep the nation calm, named a court of inquiry to investigate the *Maine* disaster. The Spanish government quickly appointed its own committee to probe the matter, hoping to appease the Americans and avert war.

The Spanish investigation was limited. U.S. officials denied requests from Spanish officials to have their divers inspect the wreck. The Spanish investigation, which consisted mainly of rowing around the explosion area, compiled all evidence to support that an internal accident destroyed the *Maine*.[2]

The American examiners, after a hasty investigation, disagreed. They felt that the ship was destroyed by an external explosion but could not decide who or what had caused the mysterious blast. The case was puzzling. All witnesses agreed that no other ship or boat had approached the *Maine*. Also, although guards had been on deck, no one had seen the trail of a torpedo.

The *Leader*, chief newspaper of Cleveland, Ohio, took the same view as most American papers: "The explosion which destroyed the *Maine* was the result of the cowardly Spanish conspiracy, and the Report of the Court of Inquiry will not tend to destroy that belief."[3]

President McKinley considered the court's conclusions at a closed meeting with his advisors and naval officers. They huddled over the reports for hours.

Many American newspapers shared a view that the *Maine* explosion was caused by an enemy to the United States rather than an accident. This front-page of the *New York Journal* conveys this idea.

McKinley pondered the results through the weekend. On Monday, he sent the report to Congress, along with a presidential message.

The congressmen were astonished. McKinley, in spite of the *Maine* catastrophe, said only what he had been saying for a year. He asked for "deliberate consideration" and took a line of restraint and caution.[4] Congress, then the newspapers and the American people, joined in a burst of resentment at McKinley's attitude toward the situation.

In Virginia, a mob of outraged citizens burned effigies—crude figures representing a disliked person—of McKinley and his chief advisor, Mark Hanna. In other states, McKinley's portrait was torn from walls and destroyed. Some visitors to the House and Senate galleries in Washington, D.C., came wrapped in American flags to show their respect for the *Maine* disaster.[5]

The destruction of the battleship brought problems between Spain and the United States to a crisis point. Trouble between the nations had existed for a long time. As one newspaper writer wrote, "The Spanish pot has simmered for years. Now at last it has boiled over."[6]

A History of Anger

In 1823, the United States had announced a new principle on foreign policy that became known as the Monroe Doctrine. It proclaimed two main points. First, the Monroe Doctrine claimed that European nations must not try to establish new colonies in the Americas. Second, European powers must not interfere in the affairs of the nations of the Americas. The doctrine, the United

President William McKinley received a lot of negative backlash from the press and American people for his reaction to the *Maine* explosion.

States insisted, applied to North and South America and to all islands in the region. In effect, the United States was saying to Europe, "Keep out of our hemisphere."

It had not always been possible for the United States to enforce the Monroe Doctrine. The greatest breach of the doctrine was by France, when the country's troops occupied much of Mexico in 1863. At the time, the United States was much too concerned with its own civil war to engage in a conflict with France. But as soon as the Civil War ended, France prudently pulled its troops out of Mexico.

Americans firmly believed in the Monroe Doctrine. Most people felt that Europe should stay out of the "American" part of the globe.

Cuba did not really fall within the scope of the Monroe Doctrine. It was not an independent nation and certainly not a new colony. Yet Americans felt that Spanish troops on the island threatened their own interests, security, and pride.[7]

In 1854, U.S. President Franklin Pierce approved a public statement called the Ostend Manifesto. It proclaimed that the United States should purchase Cuba from Spain as soon as possible. If Spain refused to sell, the United States should simply seize the island. There was wide support for this idea in the American South since several U.S. leaders wanted to annex Cuba as a new slave state. Slavery had been a large part of the work force of the southern states. Adding another slave state would have been a way of enlarging America's commitment to slavery. The implied threat to seize Cuba added to the uproar started in 1854 by the Kansas-Nebraska Act, which made slavery possible in two new U.S. territories. Antislavery forces strongly opposed the Ostend idea, and the Ostend Manifesto added to the growing conflict over slavery between the North and the South. Pierce took no further action to gain Cuba and the approach of the Civil War caused the idea to be lost and forgotten.

Soon after the Civil War, President Ulysses S. Grant listened seriously to suggestions for American intervention to "free Cuba." An invasion of the island might have been an easy way to draw attention away from hard economic times and political scandals in the United States. But nothing came of these proposals.

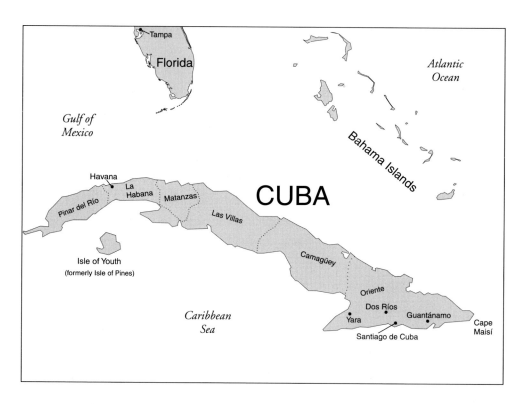

This map depicts the island of Cuba, just off the coast of Florida.

Tyrannical Spanish government and cruel repression drove the Cubans to revolt between 1868 and 1878 in what became known as the Ten Years' War. Revolution broke out again in 1895. The Cuban patriot Jose Marti, who had written reports for the *New York Sun,* was killed in a battle of this revolt, further arousing American anger.

Cuba was ruled directly by Spain through the appointment of a series of governors known as "captains-general." They were actually dictators; Cubans were given no real voice in their own government. At times, bands of Spanish soldiers roamed the island burning and looting. Slavery was not completely abolished until 1886. From time to time, the Spanish government promised reforms, but progress existed more on paper than in actual life.

Some people in the United States wanted to replace Spanish control with strong American influence on the island. Other Americans remembered their nation's Revolutionary War against England and sympathized with the Cubans. In the United States, there was a vague but genuine desire to free Cuba.

In addition, countless Americans were enraged over the cruelty of General Valeriano Weyler, who had been sent from Spain to suppress the Cuban rebels. Weyler's measures were ruthless. He was known for herding much of the island's population into prison camps and committing massacres in many villages. American anger, fanned by gruesome accounts of such incidents in newspapers, finally forced the man now known as Weyler the Butcher from Cuba.

Jose Marti, a famous Cuban patriot and writer, died in battle against Spanish forces, May 19, 1895, while pursuing his dream of Cuban independence.

Other Americans had different interests. Certain businessmen saw profits to be earned on the island, while a few were angry about money they had lost in Cuba because of the revolt. Sugarcane plantations, some owned by Americans, now stood unused. A few had been burned by revolutionary guerrillas—badly equipped, ill-trained, and often hungry bands of fighters—seeking Cuban independence.

American publishers such as Joseph Pulitzer and William Randolph Hearst viewed the Cuban struggle as an opportunity to sell vast numbers of newspapers. Their papers covered the front-pages with exaggerated tales of horror from Cuba. (Their papers were often called "yellow journals" because of the cheap yellowish paper they were first printed on. Later the term came to refer to any sensational newspaper written to shock readers.)

To make the Cuban scene more vivid to American readers, Hearst sent artist Frederic Remington to the island to illustrate Cuban suffering. After some time, Remington wanted to return. He telegraphed this to Hearst, adding that he did not think there would be a war. He received a prompt reply from the publisher telling him to stay where he was and continue drawing. Hearst said, "You furnish the pictures, and I'll furnish the war."[8]

A large group of Americans had dreams of an American empire with lands and outposts in all parts of the world. They looked longingly at Cuba and Puerto Rico in the Caribbean. The idea of an American canal across the Isthmus of Panama in Central America was

Publisher William Randolph Hearst was known for the sensational content of his newspapers. His publications were among the first to release headlines about the horrors in Cuba.

becoming popular. Cuba would be important for the canal, serving as a naval base, a refueling base, and a supply center for merchant ships. Gazing eastward, some Americans saw Hawaii and the Philippines in the Pacific as stepping-stones to China and Japan. "Manifest Destiny," a term used to describe the relentless American push westward across North America, now seemed to be stretching across the Pacific Ocean to the west and into the Caribbean to the south.

In addition to those Americans who were proponents of Manifest Destiny, a group existed that simply felt the United States should flex its muscles for the world to see before starting any military conquest. This group came to be called jingoes.

The Rise of the Jingoes

A jingo is a person who boasts of his patriotism loudly and excessively, eagerly favoring a nation being prepared for war. Jingoes usually support an aggressive foreign policy and want to dominate other nations.

Throughout history, different countries have had some jingoes urging conquest and talking fiercely about such matters as "national honor" and "defending the flag." The United States was home to an unusually large number of jingoes in the 1890s. The word "jingoism," fairly rare today, became common in newspapers and magazines at that time.

Jingoes were opposed by Americans who did not want war, felt that building an empire was a terrible mistake, and saw no honor in military strength. Such citizens were called antiexpansionists because they felt that America should be content with its present borders.

Part of the jingoism that helped bring about the Spanish-American War sprang from a feeling that life was dull. The men who fought in the American Civil War, despite all the suffering, had shared a great struggle. They were decorated with medals and showered with praise and honor. As memories of war's pain faded, a new generation of Americans longed for their own glorious adventure. They wanted to be heroes themselves—not just the sons or nephews of Civil War veterans.

When war finally came, John Hay, the American ambassador in London who was to become secretary of state in 1898, would call the struggle with Spain "a splendid little war."[9] Hay himself had watched the Civil War from the sidelines as a secretary to Abraham Lincoln. Hay had no actual experience, splendid or otherwise, in battle.

Theodore Roosevelt, who later became president of the United States, also had no experience in war. But he was eagerly looking for an army to lead, and later described the conflict with Spain as "not much of a war, but the only one we have."[10] Roosevelt, serving in his first national position as Assistant Secretary of the Navy, was aggravated at the president's patience in dealing with Spain. "McKinley," he said, "has no more backbone than a chocolate éclair."[11]

An Intercepted Letter

At the time hostilities were brewing between Spain and the United States, the Spanish minister (ambassador) in Washington was Enrique Dupuy de Lome, an aristocratic professional diplomat. De Lome had done his best to present the Spanish side of the Cuban problem to Americans, especially to President McKinley.

Ambassador de Lome had a difficult job. The Spanish king, Alfonso XIII, was only a boy, so royal power rested with his widowed mother, Queen Regent Maria Cristina. The monarchy had little strength. More powerful was an elected parliament elected by aristocrats, a cabinet mostly made up of military leaders, and a prime minister who tried to bring the groups to agreement. But the whole government was changeable, uncertain, and controlled by a small ruling class. De Lome followed the official Spanish policy of promising almost anything to quiet American complaints about oppression in Cuba. He knew Spain had no intention of really improving Cuban conditions. Words and empty promises were to be the delay tactic.

The ambassador, however, had strong personal feelings about Cuba. He wrote his opinions in a letter to a friend, a Spanish journalist who was visiting Havana. In

Cuba, a secretary who was a secret rebel sympathizer opened the letter and then forwarded it to Cuban rebels in the United States. Of the American president, de Lome wrote that McKinley is "weak and a bidder for the admiration of the crowd, besides being a would-be politician who tries to leave a door open behind himself while keeping on good terms with the jingoes of his party."[12] When de Lome learned that his letter was to be published, he resigned before it could appear.

When de Lome's letter was published in American newspapers, the letter was a bombshell. *The New York Journal* printed it on the front-page with the headline, "The Worst Insult to the United States in History."[13] Other newspapers printed and reprinted a ditty about him:

> *Dupuy de Lome, Dupuy de Lome,*
> *what's this I hear of you?*
>
> *Have you been throwing mud again,*
> *is what they're saying true?*
>
> *Get out, I say, get out before I start to fight.*
>
> *Just pack your few possessions*
> *and take a boat for home.*
>
> *I would not like my boot to use but—*
> *oh—get out, de Lome!?*[14]

One leader of the Cuban revolt said, "The de Lome letter is a great thing for us."[15] The rebels were delighted to see Americans freshly outraged by Spanish insolence.

The Spanish government sent a prompt apology. McKinley himself said nothing about the letter, but the public outcry continued.

Apart from the disrespect for McKinley, the letter clearly revealed Spain's "words and delays" policy. De Lome felt that negotiation with the Cubans was useless and wanted a Spanish military victory to save the colony for Spain. Americans began to doubt anything promised by the Spaniards.

American Aims in Cuba

The United States had said often that the situation in Cuba was intolerable. But what exactly did Americans want for the island and its inhabitants?

The idea of making Cuba part of the United States was a very old one. Thomas Jefferson, third president of the United States and chief author of the Declaration of Independence, had written, "I confess that I have ever looked on Cuba as the most interesting addition which could ever be made to our system of states."[16]

The same desire resurfaced again in the Ostend Manifesto in 1854. This time the message to Spain was blunt: "Sell Cuba or America will take it by force."

Yet the notion of simply seizing Cuba and making it a United States territory seemed to go against American ideals. Only radical jingoes wanted that. Fully supporting the revolt for Cuban independence also had problems. The Cuban rebels had destroyed some property owned by Americans. It was clear that the rebels were violent and brutal. Were they also dangerously anti-American and radical? Were they opposed to American business interests?

One appealing idea was to make Cuba a self-governing state more or less within the Spanish empire. Canada seemed to offer an excellent model. While today Canada is a self-governing nation, Britain ruled Canada completely until 1867, when Canada gained control of its domestic affairs. Britain continued to govern Canada's foreign affairs. As Canada was to Great Britain, so Cuba might be to Spain. This was the most popular solution, and the Spanish government had seemed to react favorably to this notion. Nothing had actually happened as a result, however, outside of riots in Havana by Spaniards who detested the idea.

Now, the de Lome letter showed that Spain had no intention of creating a Cuba somewhat like Canada. In fact, Spain really did not intend to do anything. Cuban independence seemed the only answer.

In the midst of the national uproar caused by the *Maine* explosion, the de Lome letter, and more violence in Cuba, McKinley had to act even though he still did not think that war was inevitable. He sent a bill to Congress requesting $50 million to be spent for defense. On March 9, 1898, the bill was passed.

A few days later, the new Spanish ambassador arrived in Washington to replace the disgraced de Lome. Ambassador Polo de Bernabe presented his credentials to McKinley, who read him a little speech of welcome. De Bernabe promptly cabled a message to Madrid, the Spanish capital. "A most gracious address," he said of McKinley's greeting. "I fear, nevertheless, that the acts will not bear out the words."[17]

He was right. Senator Redfield Proctor, a Republican from Vermont, had just returned to Washington after visiting Cuba. He made a full report to the Senate, speaking for several hours in a quiet, toneless voice.

Proctor explained to the Senate that the condition of Cuba's countryside was "desolation and distress, misery and starvation." He also described the horrors of the camps established by General Weyler as "virtual prison yards."[18] He vividly told of the poverty rampant in Cuba.

A Declaration of War

In late March 1898, President McKinley sent a stern message to Madrid. Responsibility and perhaps payment for the *Maine* could be settled by arbitration, as Spain had proposed. But the condition of Cuba would no longer be tolerated by the United States. If Spain did not change its Cuban policies and show results at once, McKinley would "lay the whole matter before Congress."[19] In other words, he would ask for a declaration of war. McKinley set April 15 as the deadline for Spain.

McKinley presented four main demands:

1. Spain must grant an armistice—truce—in Cuba to last until October. President McKinley would supervise and arbitrate any matters involving this.
2. Spain would end the reconcentration camp policy in Cuba, a program of driving Cuban civilians into fortified towns in order to contain "rebels" and deprive them of support. Spain would also provide massive relief aid to the country.
3. If peace terms between Spain and the rebels were not concluded by October, McKinley alone would settle the matter.

4. If necessary, McKinley would approach the rebels directly to ask their participation.[20]

The demands did not include the independence of Cuba. But Spain's departure from the island seemed understood in the American message.

By now, emotions and events were moving too rapidly and angrily for diplomats to settle. On April 20, 1898, after the deadline had passed with no response, both Congress and President McKinley demanded that Spain withdraw all troops from Cuba. Before this message could be delivered in Madrid, the Spanish government told the American ambassador to leave Spain.

Spain announced war against the United States on April 24. The next day, the American Congress declared that war had actually existed since April 21. It was the only retroactive declaration of war in the history of the United States.

Amid all the excitement and war fever, Senator Henry M. Teller proposed an amendment to the war resolution. He wanted the law to forbid any American acquisition of Cuba. His proposal was passed. No one at the time was much concerned with the future of Cuba, but later, this law would prove important.

A little more than two months after the sinking of the *Maine,* America had begun what many of its citizens would look on as the start of a great adventure. The New York *Sun* wrote, "We are all jingos now, and the head jingo is the [Honorable] William McKinley."[21]

Where every officer and man did his whole duty there is only room for general praise.

> —Excerpt from the official report filed by Captain Charles Gridley after the Battle of Manila Bay, May 1, 1898

3 America's Most Popular War

In the spring of 1898, Americans went to war as if they were going to a Fourth of July picnic. Brass bands led parades to army recruiting offices where young men eagerly responded to McKinley's call for volunteers. New soldiers were badly needed. The United States had a regular army of only 28,000 men. McKinley wanted 125,000 more, a quota easily fulfilled. Never had the United States entered so popular a war.

Before the hostilities actually began, most financial and industrial leaders of America had opposed war, thinking it might be bad for business. Now, they rallied to the flag. In New York's big business district, Wall Street bankers and brokers organized and paid for a special company of volunteers. Mrs. Helen Gould, widow of

38

PRICE 10 CENTS

LESLIE'S WEEKLY

YOUR
COUNTRY
CALLS YOU

R·M·WRIGHT
'98.

Many Americans eagerly responded to calls for volunteer soldiers, such as this cover of *Leslie's Weekly* magazine.

capitalist Jay Gould and one of America's richest women, donated a hundred thousand dollars to help the war effort.[1]

The society pages of newspapers even carried war-related items. Wealthy readers with summer homes in Newport, Rhode Island, and Bar Harbor, Maine, were warned that the New England coast might be subject to bombardment by the Spanish Navy.[2] Spain had a fleet of warships believed to be anchored in the Azores Islands, in the eastern Atlantic Ocean. The New York *World* told readers that Spanish ships could bombard American seaside resort towns. Fears about attacks on New York or Philadelphia, cities whose harbors were almost undefended, were somewhat more realistic.[3]

No one, including the U.S. Navy, knew much about the Spanish fleet except that it was one of the world's larger naval forces. There were two squadrons, one in the Atlantic and another in the Asian Pacific.

Meanwhile, the U.S. Navy was already blockading Cuba, halting any ships bound to or from the island. No military supplies or soldiers were permitted to pass. American ships were believed to be more modern than those of Spain. The $50 million Congress had given McKinley earlier for military purposes had been spent mostly on the U.S. Navy. Now, the government rushed to spend much more, buying up all kinds of craft that might haul American soldiers to Cuba in the near future. Tampa, Florida, was selected as the gathering place for ships and men who were eventually bound for Cuba.

Although it had been clear for a long time that war might come, America was quite unprepared. American taxpayers had always hated supporting armed forces in peacetime. Now, the army was embarrassed to find it had fewer than one hundred trained quartermasters to handle the huge task of supplying the expanded forces. Soon, the situation in Tampa turned into a complete tangle as train-loads of food, tents, cots, medical supplies, and arms converged on the town to wait in railroad yards. There was no one to unload the supplies, and no system of keeping track of them.

Tampa, Florida, was selected as the gathering place for ships and soldiers prior to shipping off for Cuba.

An Unexpected Victory

On May 1, 1898, hardly a week after the declaration of war, Americans were startled by newspapers proclaiming a great American naval victory. The astonished and puzzled public read about a battle in a place most had never heard of, led by an officer also as unfamiliar. It all happened roughly ten thousand miles from Cuba, where the action had been expected to take place.

Where were the Philippines? Who was this Commodore George Dewey? How could this victory have happened so fast?

American humorist and journalist F. P. Dunne, whose "Mr. Dooley" newspaper sketches expressed his social and political views, wrote in one column, "I thought Philippines were some kind of canned goods."[4] Americans, quickly brushing up on their geography, learned that the Philippines were a group of seven thousand islands and rocks with an area twice the size of Florida. The capital and chief seaport was the large and thriving city of Manila.

The Philippines first became known to Europeans in 1521, when the Spanish explorer Ferdinand Magellan arrived there. The islands were inhabited by Malay people. Centuries before, Chinese ships had visited the islands, and there had been frequent contact with other regions of Southeast Asia. Some of the native people were Hindus. Others followed the Muslim religion.

The Spaniards had gone through centuries of war against the Muslim Moors from Morocco, who once occupied much of Spain. To the Spaniards, it seemed that the Muslim inhabitants of these new islands must also be Moors, and that is what they mistakenly called them— Moros, another form of the word. The Spaniards regarded the Philippine "Moors" as traditional enemies.

Spanish conquest of the region began forty years later, and gradually, the islands became Spain's possession. Many of the Filipino people accepted the Catholic religion prevalent in Spain and a smaller number adopted the Spanish language.

In 1898, Commodore George Dewey sailed a small fleet of American warships from the British-controlled port of Hong Kong across the South China Sea and surprised the Spaniards at Cavite Harbor near Manila. He sunk the whole enemy squadron without the loss of a single American ship or a single American life.

A New American Hero

George Dewey, a career naval officer with a solid but little-known record, was suddenly the hero of the hour. Congress ordered a commemorative sword presented to him, and he was immediately promoted to the rank of Rear Admiral. Newspapers printed verses dedicated to him. A sculptor even made a bronze bust of the hero and sold thousands of plaster copies.

After drawing his fleet into an attacking position, Dewey had given a command to the captain of his flagship by proclaiming, "You may fire when you are ready, Gridley."[5] These words signaled the start of the bombardment. Dewey's command soon appeared in books and magazines. Young boys playing naval games in schoolyards often shouted "Fire, Gridley" at each other. America had its first naval hero since Admiral David G. Farragut of the Civil War.

In darkness, Dewey's ships had steamed silently into broad Manila Bay. There, they had waited for light. When dawn broke, the sailors saw the domes and church towers of the city but no Spanish warships. Even this early in the morning, the tropical heat was intense. Since all portholes had been closed on the American ships, the insides seemed as hot as furnaces to the sailors. One man told his fellow soldiers that they need not fear death and the flames of the underworld "for Hell ain't no hotter than this."[6]

Charles Julian, an officer on the *Baltimore,* reported that the flags of the American ships suddenly broke out on the top of every mast in the fleet. His commanding officer, Captain John Dyer, called out, "Men, let's see what we can do under the flag."[7]

The *Baltimore* steamed ahead alongside other American warships, such as the *Raleigh, Petrel, Concord,* and *Boston.* Commodore Dewey appeared on the flying bridge—the high platform atop the pilothouse—dressed in a white tropical uniform and a golf cap. He had packed so fast in Hong Kong that his cabin was a jumble of clothes. Somewhere in the heap was his uniform hat.

A puff of smoke suddenly appeared in Manila, and then a shell from a shore battery exploded overhead with an ear-splitting blast. Two other batteries on shore then began firing, but Dewey ignored them. His aim was to destroy Spanish ships. He would not be distracted by other guns.

Dewey's ships swung around a hook of land called Sangley Point. There, he saw the Spanish ships drawn up in a crescent-shaped line. At that moment, a shell, fired from six miles away, curved through the sky and struck the water beyond the fleet. Dewey did not return this fire, but moved on toward the Spanish ships. He knew he had to make every shot count. The nearest supply base for the U.S. Navy was thousands of miles away in San Francisco, California.

Slowly, the American ships moved into place. They maneuvered past dangers such as shallow water and shoals—hidden sandbars. At last, Commodore Dewey uttered his famous order to Captain Gridley, and the guns began roaring.

Several hours later, the American ships withdrew to safer anchorage, having won a complete victory. Dewey sank or destroyed all seven of the Spanish warships. The Spanish had 167 dead and 214 wounded. Damages to American ships were slight, and only seven American soldiers were wounded. Spain's eastern fleet no longer existed.

A Risky Battle Plan

This was not only a great victory but also an unlikely one. When Dewey's ships sailed from Hong Kong, a British naval officer there thought the Americans were brave but doomed. At Manila, the odds against the Americans seemed fatal. What chance could Dewey's small squadron have against Spanish forts that had been guarding the

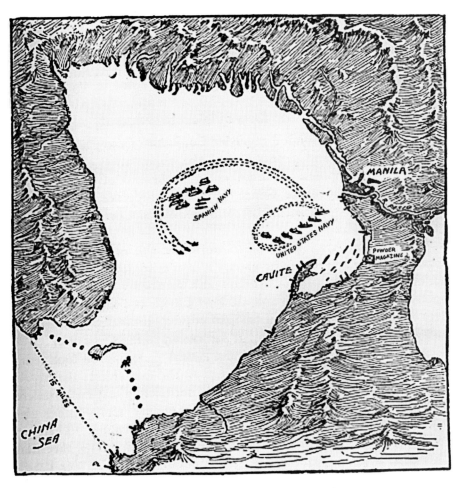

Manila Bay (pictured) was the scene of Commodore Dewey's heroic attack on Spanish ships stationed in the Philippines.

harbor for two hundred years, a fleet of enemy warships, and the dangerous minefields said to make Manila Harbor impassable?

Two years later, Admiral Dewey pointed out that his fleet could easily have been trapped and destroyed by guns from shore batteries in Manila Bay. Their advantage was that the Spaniards had been caught off guard, unready for action.

Dewey, a sailor of great experience, also made an educated guess that later proved important. It was generally believed that entrances to the harbor had been heavily mined with explosives. Ships entering without knowledge of safe routes would be destroyed. Dewey doubted this. He felt the swift currents in the bay would make it almost impossible to plant mines successfully.

He based his attack on this opinion. Fortunately for the Americans, Dewey was right. There were no minefields in Manila Bay.

Three Comrades

A year before the Battle of Manila Bay, three men connected with military affairs in Washington, D.C., had become golfing companions. They were Theodore Roosevelt, Leonard Wood, and George Dewey.

Roosevelt had served as the first U.S. Civil Service commissioner under President Benjamin Harrison, then gained fame as a young police commissioner in New York City. He now served as assistant secretary of the U.S. Navy. He was also widely known as a big-game hunter, amateur cowboy,

Commodore George Dewey, pictured giving orders aboard an American ship, was known for his well-groomed appearance.

and author of outdoor adventure books. He even wrote a much-praised naval history of the War of 1812.

Captain Leonard Wood of the army had been appointed assistant attending surgeon to President McKinley, too quiet a job for a man of action. Young Captain Wood had been a fighter against Apaches in the West and the conqueror of the famed Apache chief Geronimo. Tall, strong, and athletic, Wood was "a doctor by profession and a soldier by choice."[8]

The third friend was a contrast to the other two.

Commodore George Dewey, sixty years old, stood just over five feet two inches, barely tall enough to meet the navy height requirement. Although anything but heroic looking, Commodore Dewey was very concerned about his appearance. It was said he was the best-dressed officer in the navy, and the "creases of his trousers were as sharp as his views on naval warfare."[9]

Apart from their interest in warfare, the three men had something in common. All three craved fame and glory. Roosevelt and Wood longed to lead a heroic army to war. Dewey, bored with more than thirty years of dull service in the peacetime navy, wanted to command warships in mighty naval battles.

At the time, the three men had little opportunity for greatness. President McKinley was trying his best to avoid war. So Roosevelt and Wood bided their time and worked actively in jingoist politics. Roosevelt also did all he could to secure an important command for his friend Commodore Dewey. Through Roosevelt's efforts, Dewey was at last given command of the Pacific Squadron. Dewey went with a fleet to the Pacific and waited impatiently.

Roosevelt's behind-the-scenes role in the Battle of Manila Bay took place on February 25, 1898. War was brewing but two months away. Secretary of the Navy John D. Long, the official that Roosevelt assisted, had a medical appointment. He left his office, telling Roosevelt to take charge for the rest of the day. Impulsive Roosevelt did not waste this opportunity. He quickly sent his friend Commodore Dewey a cablegram relaying an official Navy order:

> Dewey, Hongkong:
>
> Secret and confidential. Order the squadron . . . to Hongkong. Keep full of coal. In the event of declaration of war [on] Spain, your duty will be to see that the Spanish squadron does not leave the Asiatic coast, and then offensive operations in Philippine Islands. . . .
>
> ROOSEVELT[10]

During the three or four hours that Roosevelt was in charge of the U.S. Navy, he sent out one message after another to distant commanders. He ordered fuel, extra ammunition, guns, and the recruitment of seamen. He almost put the entire navy on a state of alert as it had not known since the Civil War.

The next day, when Secretary Long returned, he discovered that Roosevelt had "come very near causing more of an explosion than happened to the *Maine*."[11] Long seemed annoyed, but he did not reprimand or discharge Roosevelt. It was already too difficult for Long to halt Roosevelt's orders. Instead, he decided never to leave Roosevelt in sole charge of the navy again.

Only two months later, the nation would be amazed by the speed with which Commodore Dewey attacked the Spanish ships in Manila Bay. Almost no one knew of Roosevelt's unauthorized part in the victory until long afterward.

Roosevelt resigned his navy position. With his friend

Leonard Wood, he now began organizing the fighting group that would become the war's most famous soldiers—the Rough Riders.

Lessons of Manila Bay

The U.S. Navy learned much from Dewey's victory. First, it was clear how lucky the United States had been.

According to the international laws that most nations agreed on, American warships could not have remained in any neutral port once war with Spain was declared. The British would have closed Hong Kong to them, and the Japanese would have forbidden Yokohama. Perhaps American vessels could have forced their way into Chinese harbors, because China seemed too weak to stop them. But this was a poor solution at best and could have had serious international consequences.

Clearly, the U.S. Navy could not operate for long in the Asian Pacific without supply bases closer than California. If Dewey had not won a quick victory, he would simply have run out of ammunition and the coal needed to fuel the steam engines of his ships.

As war drew nearer, the possibility had alarmed Dewey. The *Baltimore* was the ship carrying most of the squadron's ammunition. It was delayed on its path to meet Dewey in Hong Kong. On April 22, Dewey was informed that war might break out at any moment, and still the *Baltimore* had not arrived.

That same afternoon the ship sailed into view. The anchor had hardly dropped before Dewey had boats alongside it and men aboard to unload the precious supplies. Even while the unloading was taking place, the ship was being painted wartime gray—colorless and difficult to see on the horizon—to ready it for battle.

When the Spanish-American War was over, Americans would remember the close call at Manila Bay. Naval bases in distant parts of the Pacific would be important war prizes the United States would seek. The Philippine Islands would be one such foothold.

Spain and the Philippines

Only a few years before the Battle of Manila Bay, a native movement for independence, similar to Cuba's, had started in the islands. After several bloody battles, the rebels were suppressed by Spain, but a revolution for independence was still smoldering when Dewey sailed past the city of Manila. Americans knew almost nothing about the determination of the Filipino people to have their own, independent country. But they would learn a lot more in the coming years.

Before Dewey's squadron sailed from Manila Bay, he seized a small point of land to use as a base for future operations. This little strip, a peninsula called Sangley Point near the city of Cavite, was a major step in America's new road to a larger empire.

Rough! Tough! We're the stuff! We're the scrappers; never get enough! W-h-o-o-e-e!
　　　　　—Rough Rider cheer

4 The Rough Riders

For years, Theodore Roosevelt had dreamed of leading his own special army. He had imagined a force of cowboys, trail scouts, mountain men, and other tough outdoor heroes. Naturally, he pictured himself as their commander. Now the war with Spain gave him a chance to make the dream real.

Since Roosevelt had no experience at all as an army officer, he arranged to have himself appointed a lieutenant colonel and second in command to his friend Colonel Leonard Wood, who would actually lead the new regiment.

The official name of this force was the First United States Volunteer Cavalry, but newspaper writers quickly

53

gave it more than a dozen nicknames. Teddy's Terrors was one, and Teddy's Texas Tarantulas was another. Roosevelt let it be known that he disliked the nickname "Teddy," so the new force became "Roosevelt's Rough Riders." Finally, just "Rough Riders" was the name that stuck.

The nickname Teddy, whether Roosevelt liked it or not, also stuck. The Rough Riders themselves greeted and cheered their lieutenant colonel as Teddy. So did well-wishers across the country. Newspaper journalists began using Teddy, and the nickname became permanent.

The *New York Press*, a newspaper politically opposed to Roosevelt, nicknamed the new lieutenant colonel Teethadore because of the rows of white teeth Roosevelt displayed when he grinned, which was often. The editor pointed out that Colonel Wood "is lost sight of entirely" beside the glitter of Roosevelt.[1] Wood did not mind. He went to San Antonio, Texas, to organize a "muster camp," a reception and training post for the volunteers.

Roosevelt promptly resigned from the Navy Department and ordered a splendid uniform from a fashionable New York tailor. He took the job of choosing which applications to accept from the huge number of enlistments pouring in from all parts of the country. For every Rough Rider accepted, twenty other hopefuls were refused.

Although Roosevelt was certainly choosing cowboys and buffalo hunters, he also wanted his regiment to have a social "tone." He reserved fifty places for "gentlemen" from Harvard and other Ivy League schools, plus members of exclusive New York clubs.[2] He happily accepted a national tennis champion, an Ivy League football quarterback, and the former captain of the Columbia University rowing team.[3]

Having quickly filled the regimental ranks with one thousand eager volunteers, Roosevelt set out for San Antonio. On arrival, he saw a sign in the railway station, This Way to Camp of Roosevelt's Rough Riders.

Some of the new Rough Riders were disappointed when they saw Roosevelt for the first time. "He wore glasses," one onlooker sneered, regarding glasses as a silly Eastern notion.[4] They soon learned, however, that he could ride rough with the toughest men.

Roosevelt was talented in gaining personal publicity, but sometimes stories would get twisted amid all the various versions. It is no wonder that a newspaper in Madrid, the capital of Spain, became confused. "The Commander-in-Chief of the American Army is one Ted Roosevelt, a New York policeman. . . . He was born in Holland, near Haarlem," the newspaper told Spanish readers, mistaking that city for Harlem, New York. The article continued: "Now he goes about the country with a bodyguard of toughs, known as 'rough rioters.'"[5]

Almost three fourths of the Rough Riders were actually cowboys. Like their lieutenant colonel, they had some stubborn habits. They insisted on carrying their own weapons instead of army guns. Also, most of them scorned army hats and wore their own big sombreros.

Some Rough Riders were initially disappointed when they first saw Theodore Roosevelt, but later discovered that he was a strong leader.

Life in the Rough Rider camp began before dawn. There were many hours of cavalry drill daily and considerable time dedicated to bronco busting. In the evening Roosevelt and other officers gave educational lectures if anyone wanted to listen.

Meanwhile, things were getting rough in San Antonio. Two Texas troopers of the Rough Riders shot a mirrored saloon "to smithereens" and others shot out all the lights at an outdoor concert. Colonel Leonard Wood said, "If we don't get them quickly to Cuba to fight Spaniards, they'll be fighting one another."[6]

Then, exciting news came from Washington, arousing war hoops and a volley of revolver shots in the camp. The Rough Riders were ordered to proceed to Tampa, Florida, to board ships. As to where these ships would be sailing, the orders said, "Destination unknown."[7] The men hoped it was Cuba.

A Rough Ride to Tampa

The Rough Riders were supposed to be ready to leave San Antonio at five A.M. on May 29, 1898. Seven different trains awaited them. No one had imagined how difficult it would be to persuade twelve hundred horses and mules to board the right train car. The last mule was put aboard its train at midnight.

The trains had no passenger cars, so the men would have to follow later. A thousand men and officers lay down beside the tracks to catch what sleep they could. At six A.M. on May 30, twenty-four hours after they first arrived, trains carrying the men chugged out of the station.

They continued their sluggish journey for four full days through sweltering weather across the South. Roosevelt sent gallon after gallon of coffee through the cars. At the many stations where the trains paused, hordes of people passed free watermelons and other gifts through the train windows.

Crowds lined the tracks to get a glimpse of Roosevelt and the heroes. Many in the crowd were elderly Civil War veterans in old Confederate uniforms, waving American flags. Roosevelt commented, "Only thirty-three years ago these men had been enemies of the Union. It took a war to heal the scars."[8] Many others would comment that this new war was a way of getting over the last one. It was a step toward reuniting the nation.

Finally, on the evening of June 2, the caravan of trains came to a halt six miles from Tampa. The last leg of the journey was completed on horseback with equipment piled into every farm wagon that could be found.

If the Rough Riders had expected a welcome in Tampa, they were disappointed. No one had prepared for them. Roosevelt and Wood searched acres of tents before finding the regiment's assigned space. The weary riders pitched their camp in total darkness.

The men awoke in the morning to a surprise. Around them, for miles in every direction, stretched a city of tents. This was the largest assembly of U.S. troops since the Civil War. Twenty-five thousand soldiers were gathered on the flat, sandy plain outside Tampa. There were a few scrubby pine trees, mostly hung with moss, but no other shade.

Some men were reminded of *Arabian Nights,* a book of fantastic tales of Arabia. They stood ankle deep in sand that resembled a desert. In the distance they saw domes and minarets—Muslim towers—shimmering like a mirage in the hazy air.

It was not a mirage. The Moorish-looking vision was the Tampa Bay Hotel, a five-hundred-room tourist attraction on the edge of the city. It had five ballrooms and a peacock park.

In the hotel lived Brigadier General William Rufus Shafter, commander of the huge Fifth Army corps. He suffered from many ailments and weighed over three hundred pounds, but President McKinley had chosen him to lead the army through the hills of Cuba. Shafter was in command at Tampa because of the army's seniority policy: Important posts were automatically given to the oldest generals.

In Tampa, Theodore Roosevelt saw empty ships at anchor in the harbor with no supplies loaded. He found that the nearest railroad tracks ended nine miles away from the docks. He wrote in his diary, "No words can paint the confusion. . . . A breakdown of both the military and railroad system of the country."[9]

The Rough Riders made the best of the situation. They put on a show of fancy cavalry tactics with a line of horsemen two miles long.

Troubles at Tampa Bay

Disturbing news suddenly came to Roosevelt and Colonel Wood. General Shafter had decided to send no

President McKinley had chosen Brigadier General William Rufus Shafter to lead the American Army through the hills of Cuba.

horses to Cuba, except a few for high-ranking officers. Also, there would be room on the ships for only 560 of the 1,000 Rough Riders.

Some soldiers' dreams of glory in battle were shattered. "We would rather crawl on all fours than not go," said one Rough Rider.[10]

Roosevelt and Wood had to choose five hundred men who would wait in Tampa until other arrangements could be made. Some of the toughest men were so upset at being left behind that they simply sat down and cried.

General Shafter had been delaying the departure of the troops. McKinley finally lost patience and sent an order for him to depart at once. The general replied that the army would embark as soon as the ships could get up steam. All the ships were powered by steam produced by burning coal. Getting cold engines refired was a slow process.

The Rough Riders packed in haste and, by midnight on June 8, 1898, they were assembled with their equipment at the railroad track they had been assigned. No train came. They were sent to another track, waited again, and still saw no train. Finally, just after dawn, some coal cars came, filthy with black dust. The Rough Riders seized them. The cars faced the wrong direction, and there was no place to turn them around. The engineers were finally persuaded to back the cars nine miles to the port in reverse gear. The soldiers were covered with coal dust from head to foot.

When it turned out that no ship had been provided for the regiment, Colonel Wood jumped into a small launch that was passing. He found a ship, the *Yucatán,* just steaming into port to pick up two other regiments. Wood seized the ship. Roosevelt marched his men aboard before the other regiments arrived.

Roosevelt also found two photographers with a huge tripod and camera on the dock. They wanted to get to Cuba to photograph the war in moving pictures, which would be a first. Roosevelt, always alert to publicity, got them aboard.

The troubles and mix-ups were not over. No one had counted the number of sleeping bunks needed for the men, so sleeping space had to be assigned on the crowded decks. Rations of canned beef turned out to be so spoiled that the men threw them overboard, adding to the garbage that now blocked the harbor canal. The floating beef also attracted sharks and made it impossible for the men to cool off by swimming.[11]

When it seemed that nothing else could go wrong, a message arrived canceling the departure of the troop ships. Two strange warships had been sighted somewhere off Cuba. Could they be Spanish destroyers waiting to ambush the American convoy? No one knew. Late in the hot afternoon of June 14, eight days after the Rough Riders had broken camp to sail, the ships were finally cleared to depart. The report of mysterious ships waiting in the Gulf of Mexico had proven to be a false alarm.

The Rough Riders, without horses, now called themselves Wood's Weary Walkers. Along with sixteen thousand other American soldiers, they were at last on the way to Cuba. At least most of them thought so. Others felt they were headed for Puerto Rico. No one—not even Theodore Roosevelt—was quite sure. Their destination was still secret.

The Strange Armada

Roosevelt wrote in his diary that as he stood on the deck of the *Yucatán,* he felt he would soon help "score the first great triumph of a mighty world-movement."[12] Like other jingoes, Roosevelt had dreams that reached beyond this war. He imagined a powerful America ruling far across the globe.

Most of the Rough Riders were much too tired to worry about building empires. Others were too seasick, even though the ocean was calm. Many of the men were jammed belowdecks with the horses and mules. The mules were for hauling baggage and equipment. Fortunately, only officers took horses along. If Roosevelt had had his way, every Rough Rider would have had a horse. It would have taken another ship to transport them.

When night came, the ships' bands played "The Star-Spangled Banner," and every vessel turned on all its lights. It was a bright parade across the Gulf of Mexico, twenty-six ships strung out in a line almost thirty miles long. They ranged from modern cruisers to antique Civil War side-wheelers.

General Shafter let them proceed at their own easiest speed, making no attempt to keep them in any formation. The bright lights at night showed their position to anyone who was observing. Officers of the U.S. Navy, unable to do anything about Shafter's lax orders, feared that a Spanish warship might suddenly appear and sink the whole fleet. The navy warships, escorting the transport ships, announced their worries by semaphore signal flags and through megaphones. General Shafter paid no attention to the navy's complaints. One writer later said, "Shafter spread over an enormous area himself, and was content to let his fleet do the same."[13]

Luckily, there were no Spanish warships loose in the

Gulf. The American ships sailed on for six days and nights—noisily, brightly, and safely.

On the morning of June 20, the fleet turned sharply southeast. The troops had been comparing their course with maps. They were now sure that their destination was Cuba, possibly Santiago de Cuba far to the east or maybe even Havana.

Cheers rang out from the ships as the Cuban coast came into view—steep mountains, blue in the distance, rising sharply more than a mile high on the horizon. Some of the soldiers knew that Cuba was called the Pearl of the Antilles and was considered the most beautiful island close to the American continent.

One of the most famous of the reporters with the fleet, Richard Harding Davis of the *New York Herald,* described what the astonished American soldiers saw from the decks that day:

> Every feature of the landscape was painted in high lights; there was no shading, it was all brilliant, gorgeous, and glaring. The sea was an indigo blue, like the blue in a washtub; the green of the mountains was the green of corroded copper; the scarlet trees were the red of a Tommy's [a British soldier's] jacket, and the sun was like a lime-light in its fierceness.[14]

The soldiers had plenty of time to study this strange land lying just a few miles away. The fleet halted while General Shafter and a few officers went ashore to meet with the leader of the Cuban rebels. In a hut made of palm leaves, they would now plan the American landing and the bombardment of the coast, which would start the next morning.

When evening came, the bands on the decks again played "The Star-Spangled Banner." Then, the musicians burst into the popular song "There'll Be a Hot Time in the Old Town Tonight."[15] The Americans would start creating their own hot time in Cuba at dawn.

It is astonishing what a limited area of vision and experience one has in the hurly-burly of a battle.

—Excerpt from Theodore Roosevelt's account of the Battle for San Juan and Kettle Hills

5 The Struggle for Cuba

The naval bombardment of the Cuban coast began soon after dawn. Two little villages were the targets: Daiquirí, where the actual landing was to take place, and Siboney, a few miles farther east. The widespread firing was intended to confuse the Spaniards and perhaps mislead them about where the troops would come ashore.

By the first light, the American soldiers saw that Daiquirí was a poor village of shanties with a rickety dock. A small ironworks factory stood not far from the shore. Suddenly, a tall, thin column of smoke arose from it as the factory's walls crumpled. Spanish soldiers, retreating from the town, had decided to blow up the only building of value.

66

The American landing was an example of total confusion and mismanagement. Large ships could not approach the beach and there were few small boats. The seas were so rough that one soldier later said, "Getting ashore was like jumping off a moving elevator and hoping to land on a floor."[1]

General Shafter made no plans for unloading the horses and mules. They were simply put into the sea with the belief that they would find their own way ashore. Some animals did, but others, confused, swam farther into the ocean.[2] A quick-witted bugler blew a cavalry charge command, and the well-trained horses turned and swam toward the familiar sound. Experienced cavalrymen knew they could ride their horses through the waves. They and their mounts easily reached the beach. One of Roosevelt's two horses was drowned in the landing and the other hardly survived. He described the landing as "animal torture."[3]

As with so many near disasters in this war, the Americans were often saved from destruction because the Spaniards were equally disorganized. They had left no Spanish rear guard or sharpshooters on the shore. If even a handful of enemy soldiers had defended the beach with rifles, the Americans would have been easy targets.

At last, about three thousand soaking-wet American soldiers made it to land and formed up ranks. The army occupied the ruined village, where hardly a wall was standing. Later in the day, more men from the ships swam, floundered, and waded onto Cuban soil. By sunset, there were about six thousand soldiers trying to sleep

Theodore Roosevelt later described the unloading of horses and mules during the American landing at Cuba as "animal torture."

on the beach. Their worst enemies that night were biting red ants and land crabs.

The *Yucatán* had sailed away early in the morning, taking much of the personal and regimental baggage of the Rough Riders. Other army groups had similar experiences. Roosevelt himself was left with only the uniform he stood in and a yellow raincoat. Luckily, some essential items—such as his glasses—were sewn inside his hat.

Among the first things American soldiers discovered on the island were coconuts. An Ohio regiment had been confined on shipboard for two weeks, a very lengthy time for the short voyage from Tampa. They had lived mostly on canned tomatoes. Now, they fell on the coconuts as if they were devouring a feast.

Another discovery was the downpour of tropical rain in Cuba. The Ohioans nicknamed their first stopping place Camp Mud.

The initial major military objective was Santiago de Cuba, Cuba's second-largest city. Much of the Spanish Army was in that region. It was believed that if Santiago de Cuba fell to the Americans, the rest of Cuba would collapse quickly. Reaching it involved a fairly difficult march through jungle in mountainous country.

The first morning, the army was to follow a road about seven miles long. It looked easy on a map. In reality, it led into steep slopes where the tropical sun beat down on the men. Soon the soldiers were abandoning clothes and equipment, dropping mess kits, shirts, and extra ammunition beside the jungle trail. Quickly left behind were the woolen clothes issued by the army to troops bound for the tropics.

Cubans from nearby villages emerged from hiding in the foliage to gather up abandoned property. Revolution and oppressive military government on the island had left the villagers impoverished. They were delighted by the unexpected prizes the soldiers left behind.

The Americans now began meeting Cuban rebel soldiers who emerged from jungle paths to join in the upcoming battles. The Cuban soldiers were poorly dressed in torn trousers, and many were barefoot. They carried machetes—large heavy knives—and woven straw bags. Most of these soldiers were poorly armed.[4] The hungry, outnumbered jungle fighters had held out against the Spanish Army for years. They kept the hope of independence alive on their island.

The Battle of Las Guasimas

The first fight of the war, hardly big enough to be called a battle, took place the morning of June 24, 1898, at a deserted village called Las Guasimas. The Spanish had entrenched themselves on a ridge near a mountain pass. The roads the Americans followed led past this position. There were also Spanish snipers, well-trained sharp-shooters, hidden in the jungle on the opposite side of the road from the trenches. Their plan was to catch the Americans in a crossfire.

The Americans advanced in two groups. A regiment of regular army men moved along one road. At the same time, the Rough Riders took an overgrown trail and moved like fighters in the Old West, crouching and dodging from one clump of trees to another. The jungle was sweltering, and the men were curious about strange birdcalls they heard in the thickets.

The Spanish began shooting from their hiding places. Despite dense foliage, they seemed to know where the Americans were. Soon the soldiers realized that the "birds" in the jungle were actually Spanish scouts signaling American positions.

At last, the Americans were able to charge the trenches on the ridge. Rifles cracked, and heavier weapons known as Hotchkiss Mountain Guns roared and bellowed. Some soldiers were unnerved by the strange whistle of Spanish bullets. The buzzing noise came from high-speed Mauser bullets, standard for Spanish sharpshooters but unknown to Americans. Also, the Spaniards used smokeless gunpowder, so their shots left no telltale little puffs behind. This, too, was new to Americans.

Once the Americans were free of the forest and able to charge across open ground, the tide of battle shifted abruptly. About fifteen hundred Spaniards suddenly broke from their entrenchments and scattered into the jungle. They were fleeing in the direction of the city of Santiago de Cuba to form new defensive lines.

The general commanding the American regulars, "Fighting Joe" Young, had been a youthful Confederate officer in the Civil War. Now, he seemed to think he was back in that war again, for he shouted, "We've got the damn Yankees on the run!"[5]

The fighting had lasted only two hours, although most of the men thought it took half a day. Sixteen Americans were dead, fifty-two wounded. Soon the newspapers in the United States would be proclaiming a great victory.

The Battle of San Juan

The Americans advanced slowly toward the city of Santiago de Cuba. To capture this city, it was necessary first to cross and then to hold a long ridge known as San Juan Heights. Spanish blockhouses and trenches fortified the hill. General Shafter drew a rough sketch of the road and the defenses. He somehow forgot to include another steep

Spanish snipers concealed in the Cuban jungle foliage kept American troops delayed for hours.

ridge, Kettle Hill, which also had a blockhouse and entrenchments. Kettle Hill would soon become important.

The Americans believed that the Spaniards had twelve thousand men defending Santiago de Cuba. Cuban rebels, who were helping the Americans by scouting the enemy, said eight thousand more soldiers were on their way from other parts of Cuba to help the Spaniards defend the city. The total American force available for the coming battle numbered sixteen thousand. If the Americans delayed, they would be outnumbered.

The American officers met to plan the attack and listen to General Shafter's plans. Just as the meeting was ending, word came that two American generals were stricken with fever. They would have to be replaced. In the shuffling of command that followed this news, Wood became a general and Roosevelt was promoted to full colonel. He wrote, "To my intense delight, I got my regiment!"[6]

Everything now seemed ready for a major victory. But General Shafter and other officers had not considered how difficult it would be to march sixteen thousand men along a muddy jungle road only ten feet wide. The American advance started before dawn and continued until late at night, men slogging in deep mud.

Finally, they made camp on the brow of a hill with a distant view of San Juan Heights. The next morning would be what Roosevelt called "the great day of my life."[7] Roosevelt was now in full command of the Rough Riders, while Wood led Regular Army troops.

Bugle blasts shattered the calm of dawn. Heavy guns were dragged to the hilltop and prepared for firing.

At 6:30, big guns roared, sending flocks of jungle birds into the air with shrill cries. Suddenly Wood's brigade, which included the Rough Riders, found itself under a heavy artillery barrage. Shells shrieked and burst, white plumes of smoke shot upward from the Rough Rider ranks, and four men fell to the ground. It would have been suicidal to stay on the hilltop, for the Spanish gunners were deadly accurate. The Americans rushed down the slope to the cover of the jungle.

Rough Riders and army regulars struggled through mud. They saw Cuban rebels who had joined them falling to Spanish fire. As the Americans waded across a stream, a huge hot-air balloon they had launched for spying on the enemy was pierced by shots and crashed down. It smothered some men wading the creek and entangled others in bullet-riddled folds.

Roosevelt's orders were to charge directly up the San Juan Heights. But he found himself at the foot of another hill, the one General Shafter had omitted from his map. The crest of this rise, Kettle Hill, was spouting flame due to the fast repetition of hundreds of Spanish rifles and heavier guns firing. Kettle Hill looked like a small volcano about to erupt, fire spitting down on the Americans.

Most American troops seemed trapped in a hailstorm of bullets, while others were stalled and wavering in their frontal assault on San Juan Heights. To remain caught between two fortified hills was impossible. The Rough Riders had no orders, but their colonel, who had held that rank for just one day, immediately acted on his own.

Roosevelt rallied his regiment and charged up the unmapped slope. Bullets whizzed past them as they struggled through barbed wire entanglements. Then they were at the top, mixed with the enemy in fierce hand-to-hand fighting.

As a few remaining Spaniards fled down the slope, the Americans noticed something strange near the crest they had just reached: a huge iron pot probably used in sugar refining. This was how the spot eventually earned the name Kettle Hill.

From this crest there was a full view of San Juan Heights. Clearly, the American assault there was flagging. Some of the men who had just taken Kettle Hill began a deadly assault on the San Juan blockhouse, while others raced toward the main struggle. Rough Riders and Regulars ran down the far slope of Kettle Hill, then charged up the steep San Juan Heights. With them were African-American companies fresh from their assault on Spanish barricades.

At the same time, American troops—mostly Regular Army—were breaking through Spanish lines at a river bend near a village called El Caney. Only 520 Spanish soldiers held El Caney. They faced 4,500 attacking Americans. Still, the defenders stubbornly held their position for nine hours. When an American assault spearheaded by General A. R. Chaffee's brigade finally swept over the field, only about one hundred Spaniards survived to retreat to Santiago de Cuba. About 320 Spanish soldiers were killed or seriously wounded. Their defending officer, General Vara del Rey, was among the dead.

Theodore Roosevelt (pictured standing, center) and the Rough Riders pose victoriously on the top of San Juan Hill.

The Americans at El Caney then joined with the forces attacking San Juan in a frontal assault. In another hour, the battle was over. American troops stood on the San Juan Heights overlooking the city of Santiago de Cuba. It was another victory, but this time at a heavier price: at least eight hundred American casualties, perhaps more than a thousand. Also, some of the Cuban rebels who joined the American attack had fallen. Meanwhile, several trenches were filled with Spanish casualties who had bravely defended the Heights.

The victory went down in American history as the Battle of San Juan Hill. Roosevelt's Rough Riders overshadowed all other regiments. The Rough Riders have received more than their fair share of credit for the victory, partly because their commander was such a genius at getting publicity.

African-American Contribution

One remark in Roosevelt's recollections of the struggle is especially notable. As he led the charge up Kettle Hill, he saw entanglements of barbed wire, part of the Spanish defense. The wire was being cut by African-American soldiers who, in the face of enemy fire, were bravely clearing a way for the advance.[8] The African-American troops were at least as far up the slope as the Rough Riders, and perhaps ahead of them.

African-American volunteers played an important role in the Spanish-American War, although their effort has not been widely recognized. They were not yet part of

African-American soldiers in the 10th United States Cavalry (pictured) made major strides toward American victory in the Spanish-American War.

an integrated army. Full integration of black and white soldiers within one army unit was still two wars and almost half a century away. But African Americans made major contributions on both land and sea. Some of them were among the army's more experienced soldiers, having served in action in units against the Apache, Comanche, and other tribes in the American West. They were very strongly present at San Juan Heights. Later in the war, they served in the Philippines and Puerto Rico. Looking back at the African-American troops fighting on the Heights, Roosevelt praised, "They did as well as any soldiers could possibly do."[9]

There could be no doubt as to the outcome but I should never have believed that our ships would be destroyed so rapidly.

—Excerpt from Admiral Pascual Cervera's report of the Naval Battle of Santiago de Cuba to the Spain Ministry of Marine, August 1898

6 The Naval Battle of Santiago de Cuba

On April 29, 1898, just after the start of the war, a squadron of Spanish ships had sailed from the Cape Verde Islands in the Atlantic Ocean, bound for Cuba. They were under the command of Admiral Pascual Cervera, Spain's chief naval officer. He led a strong force of armored cruisers. The *Almirante Oquendo, Infanta Maria Teresa,* and *Vizcaya* were seven-thousand-ton, heavily armed sister ships. An additional ship of the same size was the *Cristobal Colón,* differently armed but equally menacing. Three small but feisty torpedo-boat destroyers accompanied the larger vessels.

As strong as the force seemed, there were weaknesses. American naval experts would later point out that all these ships lacked the heavier modern guns that were

79

available for use in 1898. Also, their speed was limited. In recent years, Spain had suffered hard economic times. Spanish armed forces had not been modernized and re-equipped.

The American naval commander, Admiral William J. Sampson, learned that Cervera's squadron would sail in less than two days. He steamed for Puerto Rico, which seemed a likely destination for the Spanish ships. Sampson's force of two battleships, three cruisers, and one torpedo boat could outgun the Spaniards, and the Admiral hoped for battle in the open sea.

The cunning Cervera slipped his fleet into the port of Santiago de Cuba instead, eluding the Americans. The Spanish ships were protected there by the heavy guns on the shore. Sampson's ships became tied up in blockade duty, keeping the Spanish fleet locked in the harbor.

The harbor entrance at Santiago de Cuba was narrow. Large ships had to follow a deep-water channel only two hundred feet wide at one point. The Americans devised a daring plan to keep the Spanish fleet bottled up in the harbor.

Hobson's Special Mission

The Americans realized that if a ship could be deliberately sunk in the narrows, the channel leading out of the Santiago de Cuba Harbor would be blocked. A single cruiser patrolling outside the harbor could drive off any Spanish crew attempting to reopen the passage.

Richmond P. Hobson, a specialist in naval construction, was chosen to lead a party of seven Americans on this mission. They were to sail an old but heavy coal ship, the *Merrimac,* into the narrows and deliberately sink it there. On June 3, a night with no moonlight, Hobson tried to sneak the *Merrimac* into the channel.

This was a daring mission. A small boat, a catamaran, was carried aboard the *Merrimac* to provide an escape vehicle after the sinking. One blast from Spanish guns could send both the catamaran and its crew to the bottom of the harbor.

The old coal ship moved in darkness and silence, at first eluding the Spanish shore guns. Hobson said, "It was about three o'clock in the morning when we entered the channel and steamed in under the guns of the castle. The stillness of death prevailed. It was so dark we could scarcely see the headland."

"The silence was broken by the sound of a small picket boat approaching. She fired several shots from what seemed to be 3-pounder guns. The *Merrimac*'s rudder was carried away by this fire."

"The run up the channel was very exciting. The picket boat gave the alarm and soon the guns of the ships and shore batteries were trained on us. Submarine mines and torpedoes also were exploded all about us. We could feel the ship tremble. Darkness saved us from utter destruction. The men launched the catamaran while I touched off the explosives to sink the ship."[1]

At the same instant, two torpedoes struck the *Merrimac.* It was "lifted out of the water and almost torn asunder."[2]

The tide was flowing into the harbor. The Americans in the catamaran could make no headway out to sea.

American Richmond Pearson Hobson led a small group into the harbor at Santiago de Cuba to block the entrance and contain the Spanish fleet.

A Spanish boat picked them up at about five o'clock in the morning and took them prisoner.

By daylight, they could see the results of the mission. The coal ship had been sunk in the channel, but pointing the wrong way. It had not responded to its rudder, making it impossible to steer. The *Merrimac* lay lengthwise, not crosswise, in the channel. Spanish ships could sail past its wreckage. The Americans consoled themselves by saying that now the Spaniards could not risk the narrowed channel at night.

Hobson and his men were imprisoned in a dungeon in the harbor castle. He wondered how they "were able to survive such terrible captivity."[3] They were still in their cells later when Admiral Sampson bombarded the harbor. For a time, they feared that the whole castle, including the dungeons, might be destroyed by American fire.

When the American Army surrounded Santiago de Cuba, the Spaniards released the prisoners. They made their way through the battle lines and were hailed as heroes when they finally reached the American side.

The Spanish Squadron Sails

A naval standoff continued. The Spaniards did not dare leave the harbor; the Americans continued their blockade. Admiral Sampson focused searchlights on the channel at night, not trusting the wrecked coal ship to halt the enemy.

Then, the seemingly safe harbor suddenly became dangerous for the Spaniards. The American Army had seized the high ground at San Juan. It looked certain that they would soon capture the forts at the Santiago de Cuba harbor. The Spanish fleet would be trapped. Admiral Cervera decided to make a run for it. Knowing he was outmatched, he tried to keep his escape plan secret. Commodore Winfield S. Schley, second in command of the American fleet, later said, "I knew of Cervera's proposed move twenty-four hours ahead."[4]

Early on July 3, Admiral Sampson sailed in his flagship to meet with General Shafter. The two officers were to plan a combined attack on Santiago de Cuba.

Sampson was about five miles away when the Spanish flagship *Infanta Maria Teresa* was sighted emerging from Santiago de Cuba Harbor. Behind it, at eight-hundred-yard intervals, came the *Vizcaya, Cristobal Colón,* and *Almirante Oquendo.* The Spanish squadron was making a desperate bid to escape. All four ships were firing heavy guns. Their shells went wide of the mark, sailing far above the Americans.

Commodore Schley, the senior American officer present, described what he saw:

> Our boys were waiting. The grim old vessels lay back like tigers waiting to pounce. Suddenly the whole Spanish fleet shot out of the channel. It was the grandest spectacle I ever witnessed. The flames were pouring out of their funnels, and as it left the channel the fleet opened fire with every gun on board. Shells were raining around like hail.
>
> My first impression was that of a lot of maddened bulls, goaded to desperation, dashing at their tormentors. . . . The engagement must have lasted three hours, but I hardly knew what time was. I remember crashing holes through the *Maria Teresa* and giving chase to the *Colón.*[5]

Commodore Schley ordered his flagship, the *Brooklyn,* to starboard—turn to the right. This created a break in the line of American ships, and the Spanish *Cristobal Colón* slipped past almost undamaged. Meanwhile, the *Infanta Maria Teresa* and *Almirante Oquendo* had caught American fire.

Admiral Sampson, hearing the booming of heavy

guns, was steaming back on the *New York* to join the battle. Two of the burning Spanish cruisers ran aground a few miles west of the harbor. The *Vizcaya* managed to make it a little farther but was burning fiercely. It ran ashore in flames. It hauled down its colors, and American ships sailed close to try to save its crew.

Commodore Schley, starting a rescue operation to help twelve hundred to fifteen hundred Spanish sailors, approached the burning wreck of the *Vizcaya*. He said, "I lowered my boats to assist the unfortunate men who were being drowned by dozens or roasted on the burning decks. I soon discovered that Cuban rebels on the shore would not allow the struggling Spaniards to reach land. I put an immediate stop to this . . . but I could not stop the sharks." Schley said his rescue boats "had an inch or two of blood in the bottom."[6] Losses to the Spanish Navy were horrible. The American *Iowa*, which rescued many wounded, was "awash in blood."[7]

The *Cristobal Colón* raced six miles ahead of American pursuit. But soon it came within reach of guns firing at a distance of nine thousand yards. It, too, surrendered, running aground near a river mouth.

The battle was over. The entire Spanish squadron had been destroyed. The Spanish claimed to have suffered over five hundred casualties. But descriptions of the battle by eyewitnesses suggest that this figure should be doubled at least.

On the American side, no ship was heavily damaged,

Admiral Pascual Cervera's Spanish fleet at Santiago de Cuba was completely destroyed during the American attack, pictured in this lithograph published in 1898.

one sailor was dead, and only ten were wounded—but the American victory had been full of tense moments.

The Guns Fall Silent in Cuba

The Spanish Atlantic fleet could no longer bring men and supplies to Cuba from Spain. Furthermore, much of the Spanish Army on Cuba had been either destroyed or bottled up in a siege at Santiago de Cuba.

It was clear that the Americans could seize Santiago de Cuba by assault whenever they chose to, or then could destroy the city with heavy gunfire. Since that would mean the destruction of the Spanish forces, the rest of the island could then be taken quickly.

General Shafter, Admiral Sampson, and other commanders were not eager to carry out another attack and risk more losses. They could afford to wait for a peace settlement. Santiago de Cuba would have to surrender soon, anyway.

The Americans began to look beyond Cuba to other Spanish territories. The time had come to carry the war to more distant places.

. . . We could not leave them to themselves—they were unfit for self-government—and they would soon have anarchy and misrule worse than Spain's was. . . .

—President William McKinley giving reasons for the United States to keep the Philippines

7 Americans on the Spanish Islands

After the two victories in Cuba, Americans turned their attention to other Spanish island possessions, especially to Puerto Rico and the Philippines.

In Cuba, many Americans felt that they were rescuing people who had already been rebelling against a cruel European government. There could be no such reasoning or excuse for the conquest of Puerto Rico. The island was at peace. But since the United States was already at war with Spain, it seemed logical to many Americans to seize Spanish possessions. Also, the victories in Cuba had so delighted Americans that they were in no mood to object strongly about further American expansion.

Puerto Rico, which is about three times the size of Rhode Island, was first seen by Europeans in 1493, when Columbus arrived. Although it had a large native population, Columbus claimed it for the Spanish Crown in the names of King Ferdinand and Queen Isabella. The explorer stayed only briefly, then sailed on to the larger island of Santo Domingo.

On his second voyage to the Americas, Columbus brought Spaniards with him, who founded a colony on Santo Domingo. Fifteen more years passed before the Spanish nobleman Juan Ponce de Leon came to Puerto Rico from Santo Domingo in 1508. He discovered the beautiful bay now known as San Juan Harbor.

It was such a good harbor, and the land around it was so lush, that the explorer named it *Puerto Rico*, or "rich port" in English. Eventually the whole island, not just the harbor, was called that. Later, English-speaking people were puzzled by the Spanish spelling and shifted it to "Porto Rico." Congress changed the name back to the Spanish version in 1932.

Early Spanish colonists began exploring the island for gold, without much success. The natives of the island were of a group called Borinquen Indians, peaceful farmers related to the native people of North America and Central America. They welcomed the Spanish strangers. It is uncertain how large the population was. The largest estimate is over half a million people, but perhaps their number was much smaller.

The Spanish, eager to acquire gold, enslaved the natives and forced them to work hard in mining

Juan Ponce de Leon, a Spanish explorer and nobleman, discovered Puerto Rico's San Juan Harbor.

attempts. Many of the Borinquen Indians died toiling in the tropical sun, digging in the hills, or washing gravel in streams. Others escaped, becoming enemies of the Spaniards. War and further enslavement followed. In 1582, the last surviving native died as a slave.

Having killed off the natives, the Spaniards imported Africans to replace them. Despite forced labor, the island did not prosper. Hurricanes destroyed plantations; warlike Carib people from other islands raided the colony; and eventually, English, Dutch, and French pirates attacked.

The Spaniards built forts at the harbor to repel pirate raids, including a landing by the English privateer Sir Francis Drake. Eventually, the pirates left the Caribbean. Peace was made.

Puerto Rico continued to be a Spanish colony. Impressive churches and public buildings were constructed. San Juan became a large city and so did San Germán, the island's second-largest town, although it was completely burnt by the French during one attempted invasion.

The island became highly aware of the war between Spain and the United States in May 1898, when Admiral Sampson appeared off San Juan searching for a Spanish fleet. No Spanish warships were to be found, but American forces fired some heavy guns at the castle guarding the harbor. This did almost no damage, and Sampson sailed away.

American ground forces landed on the southern part of the island on July 25, under command of General

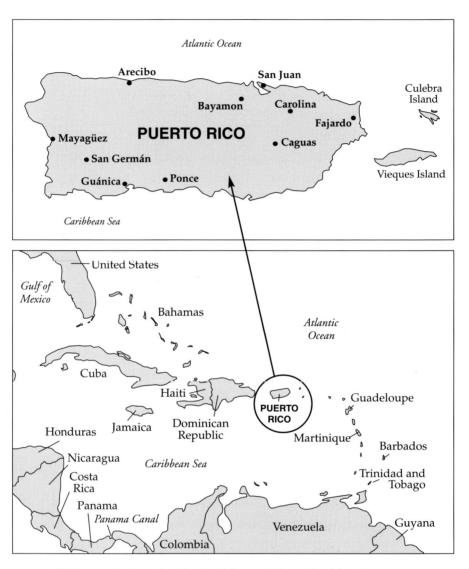

This map depicts the island of Puerto Rico. The island's name, which means "rich port," developed because of the fertile land around San Juan Harbor.

Nelson A. Miles. The first landing place not only surprised the Spaniards, but the Americans as well. Miles was supposed to be going to a port called Fajardo. On his second day at sea, he suddenly changed his mind and headed for a different place, Guánica, a small town at the opposite end of the island. Russell Alger, secretary of the Navy, learned of the change only when he read the newspapers the next day. He rushed frantically to redirect supplies and reinforcements.

Among the first troops to arrive were some Rough Riders, who had been stranded in Tampa when General Shafter limited their regiment's transport to Cuba. One said, "We thought that we would at last get to Cuba, better late than never. It was not to be. We sailed to Porto Rico, trying to cheer ourselves up with the hope of a good fight there."[1] For the time being, these eager warriors were disappointed. They landed with no fight at all— except against rough waves and rocking boats.

The people of Puerto Rico had no intention of fighting a war with the Americans. They neither helped nor hindered the American invasions, but stayed carefully neutral as the Spanish Army retreated into the hills and jungles.

American troops occupied the entire south coast of the island with no resistance. Opposition came only when the army moved northward into rougher country. "It was mostly snipers among the trees," said one soldier. "We never saw anything like an army."[2]

The first major town to be taken was Ponce. In a naval attack before the troops entered, four Americans were killed. The small Spanish garrison retreated north.

After quite a grand entrance into the town, General Miles summoned the residents of Ponce and made a speech. He said that he had come to liberate the people of Puerto Rico and give them the advantages of his enlightened civilization. In reality, the residents had been civilized for several centuries.

General Miles planned a four-pronged operation to subdue the entire island. He mapped a seventy-mile advance along a good road to reach San Juan, the capital. Meanwhile, naval vessels were standing off the coast. The American warship *Newark*, with supporting vessels, bombarded the port of Manzanillo.

Miles encountered some Spanish skirmishers as he moved closer to San Juan. The other three troop columns also moved ahead, facing little opposition. There was never a real battle or siege.

On August 12, word reached the island that the American and Spanish governments had signed an armistice. Total American casualties included three dead and forty wounded while Spanish casualties were about ten times as great. The conquest of Puerto Rico was over and America held control. The people resumed their daily occupations, having been little disturbed by the war.

Action in the Pacific

Admiral Dewey's sailors in the Philippines had been left holding a small strip of land after the American naval victory at Manila Bay. On May 7, 1889, Dewey sent a telegraph to Washington, D.C., to report that he controlled the bay completely and could take the city of Manila at any time if additional troops were sent.[3]

America really did not know anything about these Pacific islands. It was said that even President McKinley had to look at a globe of the world before he could identify them.

Major General Wesley Merritt was given command of the U.S. Navy's Pacific operation. On May 25, he sent Brigadier General T. M. Anderson out from San Francisco with 2,491 men. This seemed like hardly more than a gesture, since Anderson said he needed fourteen thousand soldiers to do the job in the Philippines. Later, he changed his mind and asked for twenty thousand.

Meanwhile, the U.S. Army was scrambling to find men to send to Asia. Gradually soldiers were assembled, until at last eleven thousand were dispatched to the far-away islands.

On June 20, on the first ships sailing east, Anderson paused long enough to seize the island of Guam, a Spanish possession in the western Pacific Ocean some five thousand miles off the coast of Hawaii. The U.S. Navy wanted this small island for a supply base at the edge of the Western Pacific. There was no resistance at Guam, once the puzzled governor understood what was happening. No one had warned him to expect an American landing.

On June 30, Anderson's troops arrived in Manila Bay and joined Dewey's occupying force. Within another month there were eleven thousand American troops at Manila, and another five thousand on the way across the

U.S. General T. M. Anderson seized the island of Guam (pictured) on his way to Manila Bay. Guam would serve as a supply base while U.S. forces remained in the Philippines.

Pacific. Admiral Dewey and General Merritt were ready to begin the conquest of the Philippines.

Mysterious Islands

In one respect, the Philippines were like Cuba. Both Spanish colonies had vigorous movements for independence, and both had been in rebellion long before Americans arrived on the scene.

The Philippine Islands were not a united country. Filipinos lived scattered among more than seven thousand islands. They spoke several different languages and followed differing religious teachings. Still, a longing for an independent nation was slowly asserting itself, especially among the well-educated younger generation.

The first violence of the independence movement took place in 1872. Two hundred soldiers—Filipinos in the service of Spain—mutinied and raised the cry of independence at Cavite Arsenal. After their revolt failed, executions and long prison sentences were dealt out by the Spaniards.

A full-scale revolution exploded in 1896, centered in Cavite province on Luzon, the largest of the islands and the site of Manila. Among the leaders was Emilio Aguinaldo.

Although the fighting between Spaniards and Filipinos was far from over, the rebels declared independence on June 12, 1898. Aguinaldo would be the country's first president. On that date, the American invasion fleet was sailing between San Francisco and Guam. When the Americans landed in the Philippines, war was already raging there. Even earlier, when Dewey entered Manila Bay, the Philippine capital was already under partial siege by rebels.

People in the United States looked upon Filipino affairs as a remote mystery. They seemed uninterested in islands half a world away. Besides, the Filipinos were racially and religiously different from most Americans. This was troublesome because anti-Asiatic prejudice was widespread in the United States at the end of the nineteenth century.[4]

The American government ordered its commanders in the islands to avoid cooperation with Aguinaldo and his rebels.[5] It soon became clear that while the American government wanted the Cubans to have independence, it was opposed to the same idea in the Philippines. No such thing was announced by the McKinley administration until much later, and nothing about the two different policies appeared in American newspapers at the time. But, everything that was happening showed that there was one standard for Cuba and another for the Philippines.

The Fall of Manila

Aguinaldo was not happy about the arrival of the Americans. He had plans to capture Manila with his own army. General Anderson reported that the Filipino leader seemed suspicious and not at all friendly.[6]

Anderson established a landing place he named Camp Dewey. It was three miles from Manila and just behind the lines of the rebel army, which was already besieging the city.

Emilio Aguinaldo, one of the leaders during the Philippine revolution against Spanish rule, became the country's first president.

The Spanish Army holding Manila had thirteen thousand soldiers centered in what was known as "Old Manila." This large part of the city was practically a fortress. The Pasig River protected the north side. Blockhouses, walls, and trenches defended the other three sides.

The city was short of food and water. Also, morale had been weakened by reports of Spanish defeats in Cuba and the sinking of Spanish ships. Thousands of rebels encircled the city, and now a large American Army had arrived.

General Merritt, the chief commander, arrived just before the end of July and announced a purely American attack on Manila. He wanted to ignore the rebels. This was difficult, for they were everywhere. He had to deal with them, but he kept his cooperation with them to a minimum.

Merritt and Dewey sent a joint message to the Spanish commander, General Fermin Jaudenes. Unless he surrendered, they would bombard the city from both land and sea, then assault it. After delays and messages back and forth, the Americans attacked on August 13. The Spaniards could have put up a strong, but doomed, resistance. Wisely, they surrendered after only a token defense.

The war against Spain in the Philippines was over. America had suffered losses of 20 killed, plus 105 men reported wounded. The United States had conquered a land that was a little larger than the state of Colorado. They had only conquered it on paper, though. In reality, the Filipino people would soon have more to say about the matter.

Major General Wesley Merritt wanted only American soldiers (pictured entrenched in the Philippines) involved in the attack on Manila.

American military forces began their attack against Manila on August 13, 1898. Flags were displayed to indicate the army advance to the American Navy, which was waiting in the harbor.

The End of the War

On August 12, 1898, the United States and Spain agreed to a cease-fire. Almost four months would pass before a final agreement between the two countries was reached. What became known as the Treaty of Paris was concluded on December 10. Diplomatic formalities and details would drag on until the following April, eight months after hostilities actually ended.

In the end, Spain agreed to grant Cuba independence, give Puerto Rico and Guam to the United States, and sell the Philippines to the United States for $20 million. In addition, Hawaii was made an American territory.

Isolation is no longer possible or desirable. God and man have linked the nations together. No nation can longer be indifferent to any other. . . .

—President William McKinley, previously a supporter of isolationism, six months after his second inauguration (1900)

8 The New American Empire

It seemed for a time that the U.S. War Department found it easier to get into a war than to end one. Although there was no more fighting in Cuba, the officials in Washington were hesitant about bringing the American Army home. Weeks went by with no action.

In Cuba, General Shafter summoned all his officers to a meeting to discuss health problems. Malaria, yellow fever, and typhoid were known to be rampant in Cuba during the summer season, and now the weather was growing increasingly hotter and wetter every day. It was a wise time to leave Cuba.

A letter of protest would have to be written to the highest authorities. The army officers, however, worried

103

about their future careers if they wrote a complaint. Theodore Roosevelt ended up composing the protest, and everyone present signed it.

The Round Robin Letter, so called because of all the signatures, angered President McKinley and enraged Secretary of War Russell Alger. The secretary struck back by publishing private letters that Roosevelt had written to him, bragging about the Rough Riders. Although McKinley scowled and Alger fumed, within three days the American troops were ordered to sail for Montauk, New York. Troops were to be discharged. The action in Cuba was over.

Despite charges that Roosevelt was boastful and condescending, his political future seemed bright because of the war. He had become "the most famous man in America."[1] Soon, he would be elected governor of New York. He was elected vice president of the United States, when William McKinley was reelected to serve a second term as president.

On September 6, 1901, McKinley was shot in Buffalo, New York, and died eight days later. Roosevelt was then elevated to the highest office in the nation, becoming the youngest president to that date.

Meanwhile, the stormy process of creating a treaty with Spain had started. Jingoes in Congress were shouting their demands for an American empire. More cautious Americans warned against too much participation in worldwide affairs. Slowly and angrily, compromises were made.

Cuba

The future of Cuba was perhaps the easiest matter to settle. Before the war began, Congress had declared that America would not seize the island. This had been put into law. Yet some Americans, especially jingoes, resisted letting Cuba go. Politicians who wanted to build an empire belittled the long and bitter struggle the Cubans had waged to have their own nation.

Finally, it was decided that Cuba would in fact become independent. This had been agreed to in the Treaty of Paris, which had ended the war in 1898. But American troops continued to occupy the island until 1902.

These American troops did much to improve public health in Cuba. Yellow fever had long been a problem there. Walter Reed, an American army surgeon serving in Havana, explained that the deadly disease was spread by mosquitoes. In a joint effort with Cubans, the army helped control the population of disease-spreading insects. In other projects, clinics were founded and water supplies were made safer. Army engineers also helped with rebuilding the war-torn country. When the American troops left in 1902, they held on to only a naval base in Cuba.

Platt Amendment

In 1902, Congress adopted the Platt Amendment and required Cuba to include its provisions in the Cuban constitution. This law attached major conditions to Cuban independence. Strict limitations were placed on the ability of the Cuban government to borrow money.

Cuba would have to lease naval stations to the United States and would have to continue the health and sanitation projects started by the American Army. More important and aggravating to the Cubans was the claim that the United States had a right to interfere in Cuban affairs whenever it thought necessary. One Cuban journalist wrote, "The Americans have made our country free. As free as a dog on a leash."[2] This had more than a grain of truth in it.

The Platt Amendment was revoked in 1932. But America kept a naval base at Guantánamo. American financial interests controlled much of Cuba with heavy investments, especially in the sugar industry and the rum distillation industry. Later, Americans would also put money into tourist resorts.

Cuban democracy followed an unsteady course. After four years of calm and prosperity, the first Cuban president, Tomas Estrada Palma faced widespread revolt after an election marked by fraud and violence. He appealed to the United States to intervene since the island was in disorder. Estrada Palma resigned in 1908, and in September of that year American troops landed. The rebellion halted, a temporary government was set up, and the American soldiers left on April 1, 1909.

A republic modeled on the United States struggled to improve conditions for four years. Then American troops, this time Marines, returned in 1912 when what has been called a "race war" broke out.[3] African-Cuban sugarcane workers had revolted against plantation owners, many of whom were Americans and Europeans.

The impoverished condition of farm workers in Cuba was a recurring problem. Although Americans intervened in Cuban affairs in many ways, they avoided the basic problem of workers' rights. Poor people in Cuba remained in terrible poverty and lacked education.

In the years between 1912 and 1933, Cuba enjoyed a few periods of peace and prosperity broken by years of economic depression and political unrest, often bringing riots and general strikes. After an especially bloody revolt in 1933, a military leader, Colonel Carlos Mendieta, was proclaimed president of Cuba by most of the quarreling groups on the island. The United States promptly recognized his government.

Colonel Mendieta gave broad powers to his chief of staff, General Fulgencio Batista. Soon Batista seized the government. When students and workers revolted against the repeated postponement of elections, Batista suppressed the uprising harshly, openly becoming the dictator of Cuba. The United States now recognized his government.

The next years, 1934 until 1959, were marked by corruption and tyranny. Cuban officials, led by Batista, were often partners with international gangsters and crime bosses. Freedom of speech and press were denied on the island, while police brutality broke up workers' strikes and protests.

In 1959, a young military officer named Fidel Castro took power through armed revolt. Castro, the son of a prominent Cuban family, headed a band of revolutionary guerrillas who had been driven from Cuba at one point.

Regrouping his forces in Mexico, a country hostile to the dictator Batista, Castro returned to Cuba with a small force. This time he triumphed, with the support of a large majority of Cubans.

The bearded Castro, usually photographed in a rumpled army uniform, was at first hailed by Cubans and many Americans as the restorer of Cuban democracy. But he soon suppressed the Cuban constitution. Thousands of his political opponents fled the island, most of them seeking refuge in Florida.

In April 1961, Cuban exiles supported by the United States attempted to invade their homeland. They were defeated in a struggle known as the Bay of Pigs.

Fidel Castro sought military and economic support from the Soviet Union. In exchange for financial payments, he sent Cuban soldiers to aid Soviet-sponsored war in Africa and Soviet-backed revolutionary efforts in Latin America. America denounced Castro's political system as communism and took measures against the island, sharply limiting trade and travel between the United States and Cuba.

The hostility between the two countries reached a danger point in 1962 during the Cuban Missile Crisis. In October of that year, the United States learned that the Soviet Union had secretly installed missiles in Cuba, after Cuban leaders became convinced that the United States was planning to attack their country. The missiles could have been used to launch nuclear attacks on American cities. American officials blockaded the island to stop further shipment of Soviet arms. The Soviet

At first, Fidel Castro (pictured) was credited with restoring Cuban democracy after overthrowing Fulgencio Batista. He soon began to suppress the rights stated in the Cuban constitution, however.

The Soviet missiles in Cuba could have easily reached much of the United States.

ships withdrew, avoiding the conflict. The Soviet Union offered to remove the missiles if the United States would promise not to invade Cuba. It later said that it would not remove the missiles unless the United States dismantled American military bases in Turkey. Turkey was an American ally bordering the Soviet Union. Kennedy agreed publicly to the first Soviet proposal but also sought a private agreement to quietly remove all U.S. nuclear missiles from Turkey in exchange for the removal of the Soviet missiles from Cuba. On October 28, Soviet leader Nikita Khrushchev accepted Kennedy's offer, ending the crisis. This crisis is generally regarded as a close brush with nuclear war between the United States and the Soviet Union.

Twenty-nine years later, in 1990, the collapse of the Soviet Union was a heavy blow to the Castro government. Cuba had been receiving Soviet support in money, arms, resources, and technical skill. Since then, Cuba has been having an even harder time than before.

The Castro government has often been denounced by American leaders as communist. Communism is an economic system in which all means of production—land, mines, factories, railroads, and businesses—are owned by the people, private property does not exist, and all goods and services are shared equally. Fidel Castro ordinarily uses the word "socialist" to describe the system he has imposed on the island. Socialism is an economic system in which the factors of production are owned by the public and operate for the welfare of all. Some Latin American journalists who have studied Cuba feel that the government is in many ways socialist. They claim that the Cuban government has some communist ideals but is mostly a system devised from year to year by Castro himself. It survives because of personal loyalty felt by many Cubans toward Castro.

Castro has been successful in increasing literacy and improving medical care for most Cubans. He has done less well in other efforts. Democratic institutions—such as open elections, freedom of speech, and other liberties—have been suppressed. Contrary to official propaganda, there are great inequalities in food, housing, and leisure activities among the Cuban people.

Puerto Rico

Unlike Cuba and the Philippines, Puerto Rico had no strong native movement for independence from Spain at the time of the Spanish-American War. The United States annexed (took ownership of) the island in 1898.

After other attempts to govern Puerto Rico, Congress passed the Jones Act in 1917. This act granted American citizenship to Puerto Ricans and allowed some measure of self-government. But the problems of the overcrowded island were far from solved. Natural disasters such as hurricanes have plagued Puerto Rico. Its exports, which include sugar, coffee, rum, and fruits, have often suffered from unfavorable world economic conditions. Recently, light industries such as needlework and plastic products have grown.

Some of the hardships have been relieved by emigration to the mainland United States. Many of the emigrants have kept close ties to their homeland while living in the United States. Some return to Puerto Rico annually. Many maintain strong traditions of language, religion, family, and social customs.

In national elections, Puerto Ricans have solidly rejected both independence from the United States and a proposal for statehood within the United States. Yet a small but strong movement for independence has existed for decades. The island remains a largely self-governing territory of the United States.

Hawaii

The Hawaiian Islands were not at stake in the Spanish-American War. However, they became part of the United States almost as a by-product of the conflict.

For a long time, these Pacific islands were known as the Sandwich Islands. They were named for an English nobleman, the Earl of Sandwich. In 1803, Hawaii became an independent kingdom. This continued until the overthrow of Queen Liliuokalani in 1893. A republic that was in part controlled by American business interests lasted from 1893 until 1898. Its first president was S. B. Dole, whose name many Americans recognize from his family's business, Dole Pineapple.

The first "democratic" government was largely in the hands of foreign plantation owners and food exporters—mostly Americans. American-Christian missionaries were also prominent.

The United States annexed Hawaii at the request of the island legislature in 1898. This was in keeping with the empire-building spirit of America at the time. Also, the fine harbors of Hawaii afforded excellent supply stations for American ships bound for Asia.

At the time of American annexation, there was some talk on the floor of Congress about possible statehood for Hawaii. Some members of Congress ridiculed the idea, insisting that Hawaiian representatives coming to Washington, D.C., would address the Senate in pidgin English—broken English with Chinese accents—while wearing long braided pigtails.[4] This prejudice against Asian people was a sign of how some Americans would

Hawaii was an independent nation until Queen Liliuokalani (pictured) was overthrown in 1893.

regard the Philippines in the near future. Suspicion and dislike for Asians, nicknamed "the yellow peril," was strong in the United States at the time of the Spanish-American War.

Hawaii became the fiftieth state of the American union in 1959. Contrary to some opinions expressed years earlier, Hawaii today ranks among the highest of American states in education, health, and welfare.

The Philippines: A Forgotten War

As soon as the Filipino people stopped fighting the Spaniards for independence, they started fighting the Americans for the same reason. Not long after his arrival in the Philippine Islands, General T. M. Anderson remarked, "I have underrated the natives. They are not ignorant, savage tribes, but have a civilization of their own."[5] Admiral Dewey agreed: "They are more capable of self-government than the people of Cuba."[6]

Americans, for the most part, did not share these opinions. Filipinos were Asian, so they were not to be trusted. In negotiations with Spain, an American diplomat expressed the opinion that Filipinos might have independence gradually as they "become civilized and Christianized."[7]

Most Americans had traveled very little at that time. They knew next to nothing about Asian people. Belief in what British poet Rudyard Kipling called "The White Man's Burden" was popular.

This "burden" was the supposed duty of members of the white race to care for and lead conquered people of other races. The idea was based on a very self-satisfied belief in European superiority. It also happened that the carriers of this "burden" always seemed to make profits, gain services, and command others.

It quickly became clear that Americans did not trust Filipinos to manage their own affairs and make their own decisions. A smaller number of Americans saw potential profits from trade and business in Asia. The Philippines had products, raw materials, and markets that were useful for American enterprise. Jingoes and certain businessmen had no intention of letting these islands slip away.

In 1900, fifty-six thousand American troops were sent to the Philippines to suppress Filipino independence fighters.[8] As many as two hundred thousand Filipinos died from hunger, disease, gunfire, and brutality in the next two years. Leading rebels caught by Americans were hanged. Not all Americans were in favor of this action. Famous Americans such as author Mark Twain spoke powerfully against the war in the islands.[9]

In December 1941, at the beginning of World War II, Japanese armed forces invaded and occupied the islands for the next three years. In late 1944 through early 1945, General Douglas MacArthur led American troops to reconquer the Philippines. But the Japanese occupation, during which many Filipinos suffered greatly, did not change the American-Filipino timetable for the independence that had been planned a dozen years earlier.

Independence was officially granted to the Philippines on July 4, 1946. Almost half a century had passed since the Filipino patriot Aguinaldo had surrounded the Spanish-held city of Manila with trenches, confident that his country would soon win freedom.

Another Look at the *Maine*

In 1975 and 1976, almost eighty years after the sinking of the *Maine*, U.S. Rear Admiral Hyman G. Rickover conducted a study to determine the specific cause of this mysterious tragedy. He was aided by various experts, including an engineer from the Taylor Naval Ship Research and Development Center and a physicist from the Naval Surface Weapons Center.

Several investigators had studied the *Maine* explosion before, but they had reached no firm conclusions. The most thorough probe had been conducted by an official Board of Inquiry of the U.S. Navy in 1911. Rickover's experts used evidence gathered from this investigation, in addition to reports accumulated over the years.

Since the sinking of the *Maine*, scientists had gained new knowledge about different possible causes for explosions. Rickover's scientific team determined that the *Maine* sank due to an internal explosion, and not as the result of a Spanish military attack. There had been a great deal of coal dust in the hold of the ship. Air thick with coal dust is highly explosive. Blasts that occur at sea and on land have been traced to this dangerous condition. Rickover's investigation decided that this was the best theory to explain the *Maine* explosion. Even with modern knowledge of explosions on ships, however, no one can be certain of all of the details that led to the sinking of the *Maine.*

A Backward Look

The Spanish-American War lasted less than four months—114 days of hostilities.[10] The American Army lost 29 officers and 440 soldiers in battle. Army deaths due to disease included 67 officers and 1,700 soldiers. The American Navy, which had fairly good sanitary conditions, lost 56 men to disease. These losses were small compared to all other American wars. During the undeclared war against the Sioux nation in 1876, Lieutenant Colonel George Custer lost more men in a single day at Little Bighorn than were lost in all the battles of the Spanish-American War.

The war set the United States on a road from which it has never turned back, although that road has zigzagged often. America, which before had tried to live more or less in isolation, was thrust powerfully into world affairs. In time, this position proved to be more costly and difficult than the leaders of America ever imagined in 1898.

The Spanish-American War did much to build American pride. It helped unite a country that had been torn apart by the Civil War a generation before. Above all, it taught the United States a lesson about finding its place in the world and becoming a major nation.

Timeline

1896—*February 16*: Valeriano Weyler becomes captain general in Cuba and orders thousands of Cubans herded into concentration camps under his reconcentration policy.

December 7: President Grover Cleveland declares limited patience with Spain's oppression of Cubans.

1897—*March 4*: William McKinley inaugurated.

April 6: Theodore Roosevelt named assistant secretary of the Navy.

December 6: President McKinley announces that many Cubans have died in government camps and threatens to intervene with force.

1898—*January 25*: U.S.S. *Maine* arrives at Havana, Cuba.

February 9: Personal letter by Spanish ambassador de Lome published in American newspaper.

February 15: U.S.S. *Maine* is destroyed by explosion in Havana harbor.

March 17: Senator Redfield Proctor of Vermont shakes the U.S. Senate and many Americans with report on conditions in Cuba.

April 11: President McKinley asks Congress for the authority to use military force in Cuba against Spain.

April 22: U.S. Navy blockades Cuba.

April 24: Spain declares war on the United States.

April 25: Congress declares war on Spain, retroactive to April 21.

May 1: Commodore George Dewey destroys Spanish fleet in Manila Bay, Philippine Islands.

May 15: Lieutenant Colonel Theodore Roosevelt arrives in Texas to train the Rough Riders.

June 22: American troops begin landing on Cuban coast.

June 24: American and Spanish troops fight battle at Las Guasimas, Cuba.

July 3: Spanish squadron attempts to run American blockade at Santiago de Cuba Harbor. Spanish ships destroyed.

July 17: Spanish surrender city of Santiago de Cuba.

July 25: Americans invade Puerto Rico.

August 12: American and Spanish officials agree to a cease-fire.

August 13: Unaware of cease-fire, Admiral Dewey and General Wesley Merritt attack Manila. Spain surrenders Philippines.

December 10: Treaty of Paris officially ends war. Spain agrees to grant Cuba independence, give Puerto Rico and Guam to the United States, and sell the Philippines to the United States for $20 million. Hawaii is made an American territory.

Chapter Notes

Chapter 1. Explosion in Havana

1. Michael Blow, *A Ship to Remember* (New York: William Morrow & Co., 1992), p. 26.

2. Ibid., p. 38.

3. Ibid., p. 28.

4. George T. Grange, *The Authentic Life of President William McKinley* (Baltimore, Md.: Henderson Press, 1911), p. 62.

5. Ibid., p. 163.

6. Blow, p. 38.

7. Ibid.

8. Brad K. Berner, *The Spanish-American War: A Historical Dictionary* (Lanham, Md.: The Scarecrow Press, Inc., 1998), p. 308.

9. George B. Rea, *An American in Cuba* (New York: Hallam & Hart, 1903), p. 6.

10. Ibid., p. 7.

11. Ibid., p. 57.

12. Sylvester Scovel, *Cuba: Our Tragic Neighbor* (New York: Johnson and Massie, 1900), p. 44.

13. David Traxel, *1898: The Birth of the American Century* (New York: Alfred A. Knopf, 1998), p. 103.

14. Rodofo Sanchez, *La lucha larga de Cuba* (Mexico: Colegio de Mexico, 1954), p. 87.

15. Traxel, p. 103.

16. John Edward Weems, *The Fate of the* Maine (New York: Henry Holt and Company, 1958), p. 71.

17. Joseph Smith, *The Spanish-American War* (New York: Longman Publishers, 1994), p. 33.

18. Traxel, p. 105.

19. Weems, p. 90.

20. Blow, p. 102.

21. Weems, p. 92.

22. Traxel, p. 108.

Chapter 2. "Remember the *Maine*"

1. Brad K. Berner, *The Spanish-American War: A Historical Dictionary* (Lanham, Md.: The Scarecrow Press, Inc., 1998), p. 314.

2. Ibid., p. 216.

3. Wayne H. Morgan, *America's Road to Empire: The War With Spain and Overseas Expansion* (New York: John Wiley and Sons, Inc., 1965), pp. 52–53.

4. Ibid.

5. Ibid., p. 53.

6. Rodofo Sanchez, *La lucha larga de Cuba* (Mexico: Colegio de Mexico, 1954), p. 152.

7. Sylvester Scovel, *Cuba: Our Tragic Neighbor* (New York: Johnson and Massie, 1900), p. 58.

8. Berner, p. 314.

9. Ibid., p. 171.

10. Sanchez, p. 161.

11. Edmund Morris, *The Rise of Theodore Roosevelt* (New York: Ballantine Books, 1980), p. 610.

12. David F. Trask, *The War With Spain in 1898* (New York: Macmillan, Co., Inc., 1981), p. 28.

13. Berner, p. 101.

14. Joseph Smith, *The Spanish-American War* (New York: Longman Publishers, 1994), p. 46.

15. Sanchez, p. 165.

16. Morgan, p. 23.

17. Sanchez, p. 156.

18. David Traxel, *1898: The Birth of the American Century* (New York: Alfred A. Knopf, 1998), p. 116.

19. George T. Grange, *The Authentic Life of President William McKinley* (Baltimore, Md.: Henderson Press, 1911), p. 195.

20. Ibid., p. 196.

21. Michael Blow, *A Ship to Remember* (New York: William Morrow & Co., 1992), p. 144.

Chapter 3. America's Most Popular War

1. Walter Millis, *The Martial Spirit: A Study of Our War with Spain* (Boston: Houghton Mifflin, Co., 1931), p. 162.

2. Joseph Smith, *The Spanish-American War* (New York: Longman Publishers, 1994), p. 83.

3. Ibid., p. 84.

4. Ibid., p. 97.

5. David Traxel, *1898: The Birth of the American Century* (New York: Alfred A. Knopf, 1998), p. 137.

6. Millis, p. 188.

7. J. R. Young, *Reminiscences and Thrilling Stories of the War by Returned Heroes* (Philadelphia: Standard, 1899), p. 24.

8. Edmund Morris, *The Rise of Theodore Roosevelt* (New York: Ballantine Books, 1980), p. 578.

9. Ibid.

10. Millis, p. 112.

11. G.J.A. O'Toole, *The Spanish-American War: An American Epic, 1898* (New York: W. W. Norton & Co., 1984), p. 137.

Chapter 4. The Rough Riders

1. Edmund Morris, *The Rise of Theodore Roosevelt* (New York: Ballantine Books, 1980), p. 614.

2. Virgil Carrington Jones, *Roosevelt's Rough Riders* (New York: Doubleday, 1971), p. 35.

3. Brad K. Berner, *The Spanish-American War: A Historical Dictionary* (Lanham, Md.: The Scarecrow Press, Inc., 1998), p. 321.

4. Morris, p. 620.

5. Ibid., p. 618.

6. Ibid., p. 624.

7. Ibid.

8. Ibid.

9. Ibid., p. 627.

10. Ibid., p. 628.

11. Jones, p. 109.

12. Graham A. Cosmas, *An Army for Empire* (Columbia: University of Missouri Press, 1971), p. 92.

13. Morris, p. 634.

14. Ibid., p. 635.

15. Jones, p. 100.

Chapter 5. The Struggle for Cuba

1. J. R. Young, *Reminiscences and Thrilling Stories of the War by Returned Heroes* (Philadelphia: Standard, 1899), p. 44.

2. Edmund Morris, *The Rise of Theodore Roosevelt* (New York: Ballantine Books, 1980), p. 637.

3. Ibid.

4. Tiburcio P. Castaneda, *La explosion del* Maine *y la guerra de los Estados Unidos con Espana* (Habana: Prensa Atlas, 1925), p. 102.

5. Virgil Carrington Jones, *Roosevelt's Rough Riders* (New York: Doubleday, 1971), p. 136.

6. Morris, p. 650.

7. Ibid.

8. T. G. Steward, *Colored Regulars in the U.S. Army* (New York: Arno Press, 1969), p. 133.

9. Ibid.

Chapter 6. The Naval Battle of Santiago de Cuba

1. J. R. Young, *Reminiscences and Thrilling Stories of the War by Returned Heroes* (Philadelphia: Standard, 1899), p. 87.

2. Ibid., p. 89.

3. Ibid., p. 93.

4. Tiburcio P. Castaneda, *La explosion del* Maine *y la guerra de los Estados Unidos con Espana* (Habana: Prensa Atlas, 1925), p. 178.

5. Young, p. 91.

6. Ibid., p. 92.

7. Ibid., p. 94.

Chapter 7. Americans on the Spanish Islands

1. Virgil Carrington Jones, *Roosevelt's Rough Riders* (New York: Doubleday, 1971), p. 177.

2. Ibid., p. 179.

3. Graham A. Cosmas, *An Army for Empire* (Columbia: University of Missouri Press, 1971), p. 118.

4. Charles and Mary Beard, *The Rise of American Civilization* (New York: The Macmillan Company, 1934), vol. 2, pp. 159–161.

5. Cosmas, p. 166.

6. Wayne H. Morgan, *America's Road to Empire: The War With Spain and Overseas Expansion* (New York: John Wiley and Sons, Inc., 1965), p. 287.

Chapter 8. The New American Empire

1. Edmund Morris, *The Rise of Theodore Roosevelt* (New York: Ballantine Books, 1980), p. 665.

2. Rodofo Sanchez, *La lucha larga de Cuba* (Mexico: Colegio de Mexico, 1954), p. 278.

3. Ibid., p. 283.

4. Wayne H. Morgan, *America's Road to Empire: The War With Spain and Overseas Expansion* (New York: John Wiley and Sons, Inc., 1965), p. 312.

5. Ibid., p. 313.

6. Ibid.

7. Joseph Smith, *The Spanish-American War* (New York: Longman Publishers, 1994), p. 197.

8. Ibid., p. 207.

9. Charles and Mary Beard, *The Rise of American Civilization* (New York: The Macmillan Company, 1934), vol. 2, p. 484.

10. Smith, p. 292.

Further Reading

Books

Bachrach, Deborah. *The Spanish-American War.* San Diego, Calif.: Lucent Books, 1991.

Carter, Alden R. *The Spanish-American War: Imperial Ambitions.* Danbury, Conn.: Franklin Watts, 1992.

Gay, Kathlyn and Martin K. Gay. *Spanish-American War.* Brookfield, Conn.: Twenty-First Century Books, 1995.

Kent, Zachary. *The Story of the Sinking of the Battleship Maine.* Danbury, Conn.: Children's Press, 1988.

Kent, Zachary. *William McKinley.* Danbury, Conn.: Children's Press, 1988.

Sanford, William R. *Spanish American War Soldier at San Juan.* Danbury, Conn.: Children's Press, 1991.

Schuman, Michael A. *Teddy Roosevelt.* Springfield, N.J.: Enslow Publishers, Inc., 1997.

Internet Addresses

Department of the Navy. "The Destruction of the USS *Maine.*" *Naval Historical Center.* July 20, 2000.
<http://www.history.navy.mil/faqs/faq71-1.htm>

PBS/WGBH. "Crucible of Empire: The Spanish-American War." *PBS Online.* 1999.
<http://www.pbs.org/crucible/>

The Spanish American War Centennial Website. 2001.
<http://www.spanamwar.com>

Index

127